Positive Safety Culture for Zero-Harm
(Behaviour Based Safety 2.0)

Positive Safety Culture for Zero-Harm (Behaviour Based Safety 2.0)

Harbans Lal Kaila
Expert
Behaviour Based Safety

TECHSAR™
NEW DELHI

Published and Printed by
Techsar Pvt. Ltd.
4435-36/7, Ansari Road, Daryaganj
New Delhi-110 002 (India)
E-mail: tech_info@techsarworld.com
Website: www.techsarworld.com

ISBN 978-93-90620-99-9

Professor Emeritus Jitendra Mohan

Message

Supportive Safety Culture is one of the essential pillars for building a progressive and sustainable organisation. Every individual's own behaviours as safety ambassadors, collaboration and engagement with all levels; encouragement, rewards and recognition for right safety behaviours make a big contribution towards developing and implementing a long-term positive safety culture.

This book by Dr. Kaila throws light on various elements that are necessary for implementing a culture of safety and will surely help the readers to understand what is a safety culture program and how to begin a journey for developing positive safety culture.

To achieve zero incidents/injuries, Behaviour Based Safety (BBS) management assumes greater significance. Many industries who are practicing BBS have achieved better results compared to earlier. The book on "Positive Safety Culture for Zero-harm" has been authored by Dr. Harbans Lal Kaila, who is a professor of Psychology and has to his credit several projects with ICSSR, UGC, NSC, WHO. Through this book, he has brought out more information to the users on various topics connected with safety culture transformation. I appreciate the laudable efforts put in by Dr. Kaila in compiling such a knowledge bank. I am confident that this book with 22 well referenced chapters with corporate case studies will be useful to all the stake holders. I take this opportunity to wish the book and its readers a great success.

Safety is like a tool, a procedure, becoming a way of life.

Dr Jitendra Mohan
President: Asia-Pacific Association of Psychology
Former President: International Society of Mental Training for Excellence
Editor-in-Chief: Indian Journal of Psychology
Editor-in-Chief: Asian Journal of Psychology and Education
Professor Emeritus of Psychology
Panjab University, Chandigarh, INDIA 160014
+91-98764-91321 jitendramohan74@gmail.com

Preface

Work culture is a deep rooted construct of a company's thought processes over the years going into daily practices. Any change in this work culture requires a well planned holistic intervention.

If you wish to really become a global company for partnering into the harbour of international economies, you have to work internally on your behaviours, beliefs, practices and barriers. This book carries a promise for you through 22 well referenced chapters of this manuscript.

No business can afford delay in safety conflict management as it amounts to direct losses of people and property. Being silent is no solution. Lack of safety culture transformation has serious implications, on one side there are gaps in safety knowledge of SOP among employees, on the other side, employees save their skin by wrong information that their organisation is best because they already have awards and certifications in their pockets. Management always thought that safety is not their job, they have to do only management, hence safety culture suffered and business didn't get sustained as incidents continued due to lack of robustness in the positive safety culture.

Positive safety culture is a game changer. This book helps in this direction. It requires two teams, one on the topmost level of leadership that is the review team, and the second team is of the top management level that is the reinforcement team, to mobilise the safety culture down to all the levels till the last person at site. Both the teams should integrate positive safety culture in the workplace culture, which is essentially a long-term planned organisation-wide intervention. Both positive safety culture and positive work culture cannot be separated as they are integral parts of organisational performance and excellence. Positive work culture would require next level interventions such as psychological safety, cultural safety, human factors, human error, work life balance, systems improvements and their integration.

When employees experience stress, they react for a change in their work culture. Training alone can help creating clouds of culture, but not sustain it. The safety professionals must understand that the business results have to be fast-tracked and multiplied, hence safety culture transformational intervention also must be on same lines involving all in the organisation.

The following guidelines would help in this direction. This manuscript describes varied aspects of the psychology of successful positive safety culture. Safety culture is an internal locus of control of the company's employees, which helps to achieve that no one would get injured at work sites. What employees do every day becomes part of their conscious work culture.

Health Safety Environment (HSE) heads of companies such as Sembcorp Energy, ONGC, Torrent, Thermax emphasized that the leaders need to mentor the positive safety culture. If leaders do it, nobody can stop this best practice to be integrated with work culture. According to Asst. General Manager HSE of Afcons Infrastructure Limited, "Our efforts are always to enhance BBS techniques for HSE development and promote a culture of healthy and incident free environment across organisation and among neighbouring organisations/people at construction areas". Business leaders who don't mentor safety culture or just maintain lip safety culture would not be favouring sustainability.

The future of safety culture brings together the EHS professionals, business leaders, researchers and digital solution providers to discuss the latest in safety innovations. Now the question is what safety culture are we following, we need to understand all interventions of total safety culture (TSC) as below.

1. Robust safety systems with digital intervention: positively reinforcing antecedents for managing all safety issues such as barriers, resources, and safety controls.
2. Safety culture: long-term behavioural interventions with fast-tracking action plan.

3. Psychological safety: do people feel psychologically safe in an organisational context?
4. Human factors in organisational cultural context: do people feel very strained with occupational stresses, workload, decision latitude issues?
5. Human error in organisational cultural context: human cognition, decision making, fear, pressure. How companies handle group conflicts and differences that delay safety culture decisions. The Bhopal gas tragedy and the IOCL Jaipur fire incident were the result of top level disengagement with the safety culture of their respective companies effecting into human error and poor decision making for actions needed to correct unsafe antecedents at sites. Human error is not personal error but in organisational cultural context.
6. Cultural safety and competency: do people feel being understood with due respect to their cultural background and beliefs, and how companies respond to these factors effectively?
7. Integrating and reviews by the topmost leaders on all the above six interventions towards a goal of vision zero-harm.

Organisational safety culture transformation strategic intervention (10 points), are as below.

1. Continued awareness to all from top to bottom by lead trainers.
2. Observers training to all with checklist, case studies, examples.
3. Measurement of at-risk behaviours by HODs at each site.
4. Steering team reviews, link to performance and policy.
5. Mentor's monthly follow-ups of safety culture progress.
6. Frequent rewards and recognition to individuals at sites.
7. Demonstrated corporate communications for reinforcement.
8. Site management involvement and BBS effect on HSE statistics.

9. Safety culture maturity (directors' review) on milestones.
10. Spot-correction of barriers and resources by BU heads.

Overall safety culture performance ranking: $10 \times 10 = 100$ marks

Finally, we need to be aware of each other's at-risk behaviours to extend support to save immediately, like if a husband has glaucoma, and a wife has diabetes, both need to be aware of the nature of each other's health issues, so that if she/he is unable to care for him/herself, it does not become an emergency, before that time, the other person is alert to support/save the person from any eventualities. Similarly, it applies at workplace/any place as an interdependent society.

Author

The Book

The future of Environment Health Safety (EHS) would change hands for safety culture from EHS to non-EHS. Managements are terribly fast in business persuasions but terribly slow in matters of HSE implementation and decision making. This differential thinking perspective makes a large space for incidents to settle in. Businesses are hard to sustain without tackling serious HSE issues, the people and businesses would get hit for sure, not coming to an end, failing all of us in our ambitious zero-harm goal. Efforts are there by some but it requires a deeper action orientation. For most organisations, change of safety culture is difficult to manage and confusing to know even how to begin. Passive management practice delays safety culture implementation at sites.

The business as well as EHS leaders are not well informed on safety culture methodology. The safety officers in Indian industry are not properly trained in positive safety culture implementation, which reflects on the institutions providing academic or skill safety training competency to them. At the same time, largely, the Indian industry is not focused to update their safety professionals except a few marginal organisations who are interested in their company safety culture for business reasons. The organisations, at large, are still struggling for Personal Protective Equipment (PPE) enforcement and barriers to safety.

This book is an effort further in addition to the previous books published by the author on the same subject. Positive safety culture means saving your company completely from incidents by involving your employees and workers for minimum five minutes a day in behavioural safety culture. Organisational behaviour safety or behaviour based safety (BBS) 2.0 is holistic, not just focusing on behavioural observations but including overall organisational/

work culture antecedents to achieve better outcomes of positive safety pursuit. It is contemporary and much needed change for organisational culture.

Comprehensive review of literature and research brought out this book based on 22 crucial aspects below that need emphasis by the organisations and their leaders.

1. *Safety, health and environment: What is lacking?:* Safety is being considered to some extent but behavioural changes are required. Environment and health are a long way to go.
2. *Future of safety, health and environment:* Future of EHS brings together EHS professionals, business leaders, researchers and solution providers to discuss the latest in safety innovations.
3. *Psychological safety culture:* Empower workforce to speak up for safety of each other, deeper insight is that let them speak up otherwise as well, for building a psychologically safe culture.
4. *Effect of BBS on safety performance:* Best BBS observers when appreciated and recognised by their company management, they tend to create more observers and positive safety culture. There are employees who don't know their own unsafe behaviours, whereas other workmen don't know how to correct their own unsafe behaviours, BBS observers help in both ways.
5. *Risk perceptions:* People think that risk is related to the use of chemicals, or electrical or equipment related and so on. But the risk is present in normal working or living conditions also.
6. *To be a global company with positive safety culture:* Companies before becoming a global entity, need to understand first that a positive safety culture is all about implementing a consciousness among the workers about the sense of brotherhood, affection, affiliation, support and spot-correction of behaviours and barriers.
7. *Resilient organisations and positive safety culture:* Developing resilient organisation and positive safety culture

is meant to raise own implementation experience, data and information within the organisation so that it can bounce forward in case of incidents, failure or uncertainty.

8. *Managements prioritise on the safety culture drive:* Every worker should prioritise on human life, make time for an observation around at site daily, without fail, look for at-risk behaviour to spot-correct in a positive manner.
9. *Passion for safety culture transformation:* Having a passion for safety means actively caring about your people and your operations. If you take care of your people, they will be more productive.
10. *A case on positive safety culture:* Positive behaviour safety or big brother safety (BBS) provides the necessary components of care and timely intervention, however, needs to be backed up by a robust safety management system.
11. *Safety culture suffers from disconnect and decision making:* People carry their positions and speak with inflated ego. Hence, they do not open up or feel psychologically disconnected with each other. Participation of employees in safety culture is less due to impaired felt leadership and dependent safety culture practised by site heads. They remain passive as they depend upon HSE officers and don't take safety ownership for their own people. This reveals a disconnect between top leaders, site leaders and frontline engineers.
12. *Digitalisation of positive safety culture:* Digitalising safety processes, checklists, training and implementations plays an essential role in driving your company's safety culture.
13. *Success and challenges of positive safety culture:* A successful positive safety culture connects everyone in the company around a common goal to measurably reduce near misses and incidents, and have huge implications for business success.
14. *Total safety culture (TSC) interventions:* A safety professional's goal is to achieve TSC in an organisation including a good balance of enforcement and reinforcements between the interventions such as behavioural safety,

psychological safety, human factors, human errors, cultural safety, and robust safety systems. TSC is the one in which every worker is actively caring for safety of each other and also being rewarded for his/her observations and corrections. TSC includes extending safety culture beyond work culture to social milieu.

15. *Linking safety behaviour to key performance indicators (KPI):* Like with one seed, we can grow thousands of fruits and more seeds, similarly with behavioural KPI of an individual employee and actions, we save thousands of lives from incidents, and prevent injuries.
16. *Human factors and human error in safety culture:* How organisations and leadership respond to human factors and human errors, matters most in building positive vibes for safety culture.
17. *Cultural safety and diversity (CSD):* CSD is addressed to see that the workers especially at the lowest level are being listened to and understood with due respect to their cultural background, beliefs and language, for ensuring development of positive safety culture.
18. *Integrating total safety culture interventions with organisational behaviour:* Integrating and sustaining safety culture require a controlled focus on several levels of influence on worker safety and wellbeing, as the relationship between work and safety is never unidirectional.
19. *Fixing accountability levels to mobilise positive safety culture:* Accountability, equality, encouragement, teamwork, and training are the five elements of safety culture. All the five work in tandem for building best work culture.
20. *Rewarding workers for safety cultural change:* Most organisations remain passive in celebrating employee rewards for safety culture, some are regularly active and integrate it to their appraisal process, yet sometimes rewards are unfair as perceived by employees which significantly and adversely affect the positive safety culture.
21. Three months E-training course questionnaire and evaluation on *Behaviour Based Safety 2.0 (Zero-harm with Positive Work Culture)*

Though the positive safety culture is the responsibility of an individual employee /worker, as well as the organisation, it brings everyone together for an active HSE drive. During positive safety culture development, organisational hierarchies turn into brothers and sisters to actively care for the wellbeing of colleagues and the business workforce. Employees are trained with an objective that they are not the tools of safety rather a human chain to care for each other which promotes zero-harm culture at workplaces or elsewhere. When someone is cared for with human touch, it helps.

Safety culture arithmetic depends upon the two organisational indicators, one is the participation rate of workers, and the second is the monthly trends rate of at-risk behaviours. The accountability of leaders in safety culture at site as well as the corporate level, is an independent factor which influences both these above indicators. Hence, people need to be not only made accountable, but also need to be evaluated on their accountability performance by their seniors.

The Author

Dr. Harbans Lal Kaila, earned Masters' degree in Psychology from Guru Nanak Dev University, Doctorate from Tata Institute of Social Sciences, is a retired Professor of Organizational Psychology with 39 years of professional experience, published books/articles and participated in national/international conferences. He pioneered BBS training in India, conducted about 2000 BBS workshops in India/abroad and is a member expert panel for National Safety Council. He served the Central Labour Institute, Ministry of Labour for 10 years and as a Professor at the SNDT Women's University for 18 years at Mumbai. He is a resource person (to organisations like ITC, SAIL, GAIL, ESSAR, RIL, Colourtex, Reliance Energy, Ultratech, CFCL, Sandoz, Tata Motors, M&M, BPCL, CPCL, ONGC, Suzlon, TUV, DNV, Bajaj Auto, Bayer CropScience, Serum, SMC, NPC, GE, IOCL, BHEL, Oil India, Privi, HPCL, HCC, Kalpatru, Torrent, CTEA, Greentech, ICC, Pidilite, Voltas, J&J, NFIL, Aarti, Privi, Galaxy Surfactants, Volkswagen, Jindal, Sterlite, Vedanta, L&T, RCF, DCM Shriram, Solaris, Agrocel, Piramal, Dorf Ketal, TRL Krosaki, Sembcorp, Uflex, Afcons, AM/NS, Hikal, Sunshield, Gunnebo, Amara-Raja, Hindalco, Ampacet, Tata Projects, Toyota, NTPC, Vaaman, Hirschvogel, NFIL, Asian Paints, Vasudha, Godrej, Thyssenkrupp, BGPPL) and conducted about 100 safety culture surveys for many locations in India. Dr. Kaila represented India in Conferences at New York, Berlin, Japan, Muscat, Dubai, Rome, New Zealand, London, Egypt, Sydney, Malaysia. He is an Editor of the *Journal of Psychosocial Research* and Founder Director of the Forum of Behavioural Safety.

Contact for any clarification: KAILAHL@HOTMAIL.COM

Contents

1

Safety, Health and Environment What is Lacking?

Government recognizes that safety and health of workers has a positive impact on productivity and economic and social development. Government must ask employers to include their company's behavioural safety score in their annual HSE index and reflect in the report, as behaviour is the root cause of all incidents. The three important OSH needs are: 1. legislation to extend OSH coverage to all sectors including the unorganised sector; 2. spreading the awareness about OSH among stakeholders; 3. development of OSH infrastructure and OSH professionals. Other issues include integration of occupational health with primary health care (Pingle, 2012).

HSE culture is the need of the hour for building awareness and behaviour. Integration of all three pillars of health, safety and environment is crucial for balancing HSE culture.Without access to any kind of formal training on occupational safety & health (OSH), the overall awareness levels in India are low. The Government of India has declared the National Policy on Safety, Health and Environment at Workplace (NPSHEW) which aims to establish a preventive safety and health culture in the country through elimination of the incidence of work-related injuries, diseases, fatalities, disasters and to enhance the wellbeing of employees in all the sectors of economic activity in the country. Several steps are taken for promoting and propagating the objective of safety and health by holding various conferences, awareness camps, safety weeks, campaigns, awards and conducting of surveys, etc. The Government of India firmly believes that building and maintaining national preventive safety and health culture is the need of the hour. With a view to develop such a culture and to improve the safety, health, and environment at the workplace, it is essential to meet the following requirements (NPSHEW, 2019).

- Providing a statutory framework on occupational safety and health in respect of all sectors a system of incentives to employers and employees to achieve higher health and safety standards.
- Providing for a system of non-financial incentives for improvement in safety and health.
- Establishing and developing the research and development capability in emerging areas of risk and providing for effective control measures.
- Focusing on prevention strategies and monitoring performance through improved data collection system on injuries and diseases.
- Developing and providing required technical manpower and knowledge in the areas of safety, health, and environment at workplaces in different sectors.
- Promoting inclusion of safety, health, and environment, improvement at workplaces as an important component in other relevant national policy documents.

- Including safety and occupational health as an integral part of every operation.

Indian workplaces face several challenges when it comes to workplace safety which can directly impact workers both physically and mentally. Up-skilling workers in health, safety and wellbeing can significantly help mitigate risks associated with these challenges (*Economic Times*, 2022).

What is being emphasized less at sites, is it safety, health, environment (SHE). How to balance?

Safety first, forget about the rest, opines the managing director of Chennai Petroleum Corporation Ltd. According to him, we have to establish safety culture, penalties have to be deducted to ensure the safety norms. The entire management's head is down with incidents, safety culture would keep your head high. There is a need to personalise SHE in order to effect the same in work settings or elsewhere. There is no fire call in the past few years, production and profits are historically high following the positive safety cultures and increase of NMI (near miss reporting). Safety behaviour observation (SBO) targets have to be fixed per employee per day and reviewed by the managing director. Keep on increasing safety conversations, do not expect results immediately. Talk to one worker about safety daily. Safety culture has to be in our DNA and daily routine, in whatever walk of life we are. We have to be a brand ambassador of safety culture to our society, industry and the mother earth. Dependent safety culture continues, hence HODs need to drive interdependent safety culture.

What is less emphasised at sites: Is that safety, health or environment, How to balance? The results of responses of industry experts are reflected below.

What is less emphasised at sites

- In Sembcorp Energy company, safety, health or environment are not being less emphasized. CEO and Independent Director of Sembcorp Energy reviews BBS every week.
- At DCM Shriram, all three are integral part of each other. Anything ignored in one will impact the other. That is the reason of having EHS management in place.

- At Everest Industries, health gets less importance compared with the other two parameters. Safety is emphasised anyways, housekeeping which is part of safety culture improves the environment. However, good healthy employees can improve productivity and enable more watchful mind.
- At AFCONS, safety is being considered to some extent and behavioural changes are required. Environment and health are a very long way to go.
- At Flourine, all 3 in a chronology of environment, safety and health are emphasised.
- At IOCL, first priority to individual safety. In overall, safety, health and environment, all are equally important.
- According to ONGC, In this brutal competitive world, all three are being compromised. Independent watch dogs can be thought of.
- According to GAIL, all three areas are underemphasised. Thrust from leadership, agile team of HSE professionals and reward, recognition and punitive fine schemes can make huge difference in implementation success at work sites.
- At SGIL, as per analysis, environment and health are less emphasised.
- According to Vasudha Pharma, in many industries, more talking about safety, less focus and implementation. Only through top management involvement, EHS can be balanced.
- According to Galaxy Surfactants, We can balance by better planning and showing safe behaviour to all safety, health, environment.
- As per Director Factories, all the three are interrelated, are less emphasised.

Toolbox talks, informal meetings amongst construction managers and workers to brief and discuss hazards, risks, and safety procedures, is an effective way to ensure safety during construction projects, which should be given to all employees every day. Construction companies should consider implementing health and safety culture change programmes. By improving their organisational culture and increasing staff engagement with health and safety arrangements, companies can make a positive difference. India should push for a culture change in 2023 regarding the way that risks to workers' health, safety, and wellbeing are managed, including during construction work. Although legislation is important in helping to improve the overall health and safety posture of an organisation, the project leaders in the construction sector should take the lead in championing the need for a good health and safety culture at every level of an organisation (Kamarajan, 2023).

Positive safety observations, risk-based conversations and spot-corrections of at-risk behaviours and barriers each day by observers would make a change in organisational safety performance. Increasing someone's safety consciousness is a human act to enhance your soul as an observer.

REFERENCES

Economic Times (2022, Mar 07). Workplace safety challenges: How safe are your workers? https://economictimes.indiatimes.com/news/company/corporate-trends/workplace-safety-challenges-how-safe-are-your-workers/articleshow/90044699.cm?utm_source=contentofinterest&utm_medium=text&utm_campaign=cppst

Kamarajan, M. (2023, Jan. 22). Improving construction safety in 2023. https://timesofindia.indiatimes.com/blogs/voices/improving-construction-safety-in-2023/?source=app&frmapp=yes

NPSHEW (2019, July, 26). National Policy on Safety, Health, and Environment at Workplace. https://journalsofindia.com/national-policy-on-safety-health-and-environment-at-workplace- npshew/

Pingle, Shyam. (2012). Occupational Safety and Health in India: Now and the Future. *Industrial Health*. 50. 167-71. 10.2486/indhealth.MS1366.

2

The Future of Safety, Health and Environment

The future of EHS brings together EHS professionals, business leaders, researchers and solution providers to discuss the latest in safety innovations (NSC, 2023). The future of EHS would essentially replace safety culture from the hands of EHS persons to non-EHS employees.

Rapidly changing working conditions, accelerated by the pandemic, new technologies, shifting demographics, different patterns of employment and work organisation will have significant and not yet fully known impacts on workers' health, safety and wellbeing. Unilever believes that every single employee and individual we work with should have the right to be able to live and work free from the risk of injuries and accidents. At the same time, every employee and worker has an ethical responsibility to actively observe and spot-correct the risks around for creating a positive safety culture from workplace to any place. Worker health and wellbeing are now prioritized as major outcomes of interest as well as issues associated with work-life fit are of particular concern (Felknor *et al.*, 2021).

A study on the future of research on work, safety, health and wellbeing (Sorenson, *et al.*, 2021) emphasised that the nature of relationships between employers and workers; and the benefits and protections available to workers, will be critical for anticipating the consequences of future changes in the conditions of work, and ultimately help inform decision-making around policies and practices intended to protect and promote worker safety, health, and wellbeing. This approach anticipates changes in the way work is structured, managed, and experienced by workers and can effectively inform policies and practices needed to protect and promote worker safety, health and wellbeing.

As the national safety culture develops, it would also impact the thinking of small businesses to think positively about the safety culture amongst their workers. As the MNCs, larger companies pick up on the HSE fronts, their small vendors, sub-contractors would also be insisted to follow the same line of trends in a gradual way.

Workplaces in 2023 will be more diverse, distributed and virtual than ever before. Corporations and even smaller organizations will learn to adapt in order to cater for shifting employee expectations in the wake of the post-pandemic "new normal", and behavioural trends. As younger generations join the workforce and the middle generations begin to move up into senior positions, they will bring new values with them. Observational experience seems to suggest that this will result in workplace cultures that are more accepting of diversity and tolerant of individuals' expectations of flexibility in their working lives (Marr, 2022).

Indian workplaces face several challenges when it comes to workplace safety which can directly impact workers both physically and mentally. Upskilling workers in health, safety and wellbeing can significantly help mitigate risks associated with these challenges. Indian organisations along the challenges are on their journey to achieving best practice health, safety and wellbeing in the workplace (The Economic Times, 2022).

Psychological safety is to be crucial for India Inc in 2023. 45% of all employers surveyed believe that psychological safety is a strong performance indicator and 47% believe it is a crucial need since it leads to higher employee retention and engagement, according to new data (Sarkar, 2023).

Though, at workplaces in an organisation, a set of diverse cultures prevail impacting employees' safety behaviours, an approach of behaviour based safety (BBS) implementation attempts creating a culture-free safety environment which is actively caring for each other irrespective of individuals or groups or occupational or hierarchical cultures.

Understanding worker health and safety in 2023 and further would depend upon "What are all the support systems that we've built into our economy, communities, and governments that help a single business have a healthy workforce and a healthy business in and of itself?"

Rapidly changing working conditions such as work from home, will have significant and not yet fully known impacts on workers, in terms of worker stress, burnout, isolation and sedentariness, obesity. These challenges, demand about work arrangements, the redesign of work. Technology is another aspect, with AI, machine learning, holographic imaging. "If you look at Uber, for example, these platforms use AI to decide which driver gets what ride, deciphering workloads and things like that. We have no clue how that impacts worker's wellbeing" (Igoe, 2023).

Worker's wellbeing is in demand as organisational culture shifts. Attitudes about employee's mental health have dramatically shifted, and psychologists are leading the charge to help businesses prioritise employee's wellbeing. Stress among workers throughout the globe is at an all-time high. Forty-four per cent of workers reported that they experienced significant stress the previous day and more than one-fifth experienced significant anger or sadness the previous day, according to data collected from more than 160 countries throughout 2021. Attitudes about employee's mental health have dramatically shifted. The trend is changing on workplace behaviour. The pandemic forced employers to recognise that they must pay more attention to the mental health of employees, and that the conditions in the work environment can either exacerbate or prevent mental health challenges. The fact that more organisations are acknowledging the important connection between workplace conditions and wellbeing is an encouraging shift.The organisations that are the most nimble and creative in managing changes will lead the way in attracting talent. Workers (71%) believe that their employers are more concerned about employees' mental health than in the past. More than 80% agreed that how employers support mental health will be an important consideration for them when they look for future work. Organisations must convey the concern to employees that they care for their wellbeing and safety (Stringer, 2023).

REFERENCES

Felknor, Sarah A. Jessica MK Streit, and Nicole T Edwards *et al.,* (2021, October 29) Exploring the Future of Worker Health and Safety in the Post-Pandemic World. https://blogs.cdc.gov/ niosh-science-blog/2021/10/29/erp/

Igoe, Katherine J. (2023).The Changing Face of Worker Safety, Health, and Wellbeing in a Post-Pandemic Future. https://www.hsph.harvard.edu/ ecpe/the-changing-face-of-worker- safety-health-and-wellbeing-in-a-post-pandemic-future/

Marr Bernard (2022, Dec 6). Future of Work: The 4 Biggest Workplace Trends in 2023. https://
www.linkedin.com/pulse/future-work-4-biggest-workplace-trends-2023-bernard-marr

NSC (2023).The Future of EHS 2023. https://www.nsc.org/workplace/ safety-topics/work-to- zero/future-of-ehs?

Sarkar, B. (2023, Feb 15). Psychological safety to be crucial for India Inc in 2023. https:// economictimes.indiatimes.com/news/company/ corporate-trends/psychological-safety-to-be- crucial-for-india-inc-in-2023-and-beyond-survey/articleshow/97937736.cms? utm_source= contentofinterest&utm_medium=text&utm_campaign=cppst

Stringer, Heather (2023, January 1). Worker wellbeing is in demand as organizational culture shifts. 2023 Trends Report. Vol. 54 No. 1. https://www.apa.org/monitor/2023/01/trends- worker-wellbeing

Sorensen Glorian, Jack T. Dennerlein, Susan E. Peters, Erika L. Sabbath, Erin L. Kelly, Gregory R. Wagner (2021). The future of research on work, safety, health and wellbeing: A guiding conceptual framework. Social Science & Medicine,Volume 269, 2021,113593,ISSN 0277-9536, https://doi.org/10.1016/j.socscimed.2020.113593.

The Economic Times (2022). Workplace safety challenges: How safe are your workers? https://economictimes.indiatimes.com/ news/company/corporate-trends/workplace-safety-challenges-how-safe-are-your-workers/articleshow/90044699.cms?utm_ source=contentofinterest&utm_medium=text&utm_campaign=cppst

3

Psychological Safety Culture

Empower workforce to speak up for safety of each other, but the deeper insight is that let them speak up otherwise as well, for building a psychologically safe culture.

Workplace psychological safety has become increasingly important in today's business world as it has shown to lead to improved performance, increased productivity, and higher employee engagement. These advantages can lead to a more successful and profitable organization (Sewell, 2023).

Psychological safety intervention is an important part of the total safety culture. Most companies respond and address the psychological safety issues of the workforce, such as fears, anxieties, depression, dissatisfaction, pressures and so on. But they are dealt with in informal ways by some sensitive and sensible managers, not as an integral part of the work system as an organisational system. Hence, the effectiveness of psychological safety measures remains ineffective and unmeasurable. Therefore, it is necessary to understand it more clearly for better mental health and wellbeing of employees so that they feel psychologically safe at workplaces.

Having psychologically safe teams can improve learning, creativity and performance within organisations. Within a healthcare context, psychological safety supports patient safety by enabling engagement in quality improvement and encouraging staff to speak up about errors. Despite the low levels of psychological safety in healthcare teams and the important role it plays in supporting patient safety, there is a dearth of research on interventions that can be used to improve psychological safety or its related constructs. This review synthesises the content, theoretical underpinnings and outcomes of interventions which have targeted psychological safety, speaking up, and voice behaviour within a healthcare setting. It aims to identify successful interventions and inform the development of more effective interventions. Mixed results were found for the efficacy or effectiveness of these interventions. While some interventions showed improvement in outcomes related to psychological safety, speaking up and voice, this was not consistently demonstrated across interventions. Included interventions' ability to demonstrate improvements in these outcomes were limited by a lack of objective outcome measures and the ability of educational interventions alone to change deeply rooted speaking up behaviours. To improve our understanding of the efficacy or effectiveness of interventions targeting psychological safety, speaking up and voice behaviour, longitudinal and multifaceted interventions are needed. In order to understand whether these interventions are successful, more objective measures should be developed. It is recommended that future research involves end users in the design phase of interventions, target both group and organisational levels, ensure visible leader support and work across and within interdisciplinary teams (O'Donovan *et al.*, 2020).

The psychological safety and its importance seems to be recognised across industries. One crucial misconception among business leaders is that psychological safety will be present in any reasonably healthy work environment, like freedom from harassment or a commitment to keeping workers injury-free. In fact, psychologically safe work environments are rare. Creating psychological safety in a workplace is truly challenging and takes an unusual degree of commitment and skill. It is a process of helping people develop new beliefs and behaviours. Building a psychologically safe work environment starts with shifting the narrative of the intervention from culture change or interpersonal skills in order to make the case that the quality of conversation matters for results. Senior executives buy into the importance of psychological safety when they appreciate its role in solving complex problems. Train both individuals and teams and incorporate visualisation. It gets easier over time because they become better at noticing positive examples in their practice of new behaviours. Normalise vulnerability related to work. It is normal to experience mild anxiety as a consequence of feeling vulnerable. Research on anxiety training shows that practising small acts of vulnerability reduces that anxiety. Ask executive teams to identify an important complex topic on which they had been unable to make progress, and thereby developing their skills and making progress at the same time. Focusing on performance, working at both the individual and group level, using visualisation, normalising vulnerability, and using real problems to develop skills while making progress on thorny issues comprise a powerful approach to altering the climate and capabilities of any team. Building capabilities related to psychological safety perspective is increasingly a vital part of achieving excellence in challenging business contexts (Edmondson and Hugander, 2021).

Psychological safety, the belief that it is safe to speak up, is vital. The psychological safety improves effectiveness of our team and is the key to high-performing teams. Psychological safety and feeling heard were both statistically significantly associated with lower burnout (Kerrissey *et al.*, 2022).

Safety, according to Maslow's hierarchy, is a human need. Creating psychologically safe work environments is critical. The term psychological safety was coined by Harvard Business School professor Amy Edmondson. She defines it as a shared belief that the team is safe for interpersonal risk-taking. Establishing a climate of psychological safety allows space for people to speak up and share their ideas. For leaders, speaking out is actually less important than how we react and respond to other team members (Jiménez, 2022).

Do you have a psychologically safe workplace? Assess and address the psychological health and safety of your workplace. Measure and improve psychological health and safety at work by asking all employees about the work situations which highlight the psychosocial factors, hazards and indicators of inclusion, stress and trauma. Take action on the results directed to the senior leadership and decision-making team to provide insight to the levels of stress and satisfaction at work.

"What went wrong?" or "How could we have prevented this?". Instead, when the manager asks a simple question: What did you learn? You understand that what he/she was doing was building psychological safety. She/he understood that learning was key for me and my team's future performance depended on it. Psychological safety is a critical concept for teams and the people that lead them (Gallo, 2023).

REFERENCES

Edmondson, Amy C. and Hugander, Per (2021,June 22). 4 Steps to Boost Psychological Safety at Your Workplace. https://hbr.org/2021/06/4-steps-to-boost-psychological-safety-at-your- workplace

Jiménez, Jacinta (2022, October 17). Why psychological safety at work matters and how to create it. https://www.betterup.com/blog/why-psychological-safety-at-work-matters

Gallo Amy (2023, February 15). What is Psychological Safety? https://hbr.org/2023/02/what- is-psychological-safety

Kerrissey, Michaela J.; Hayirli, Tuna C.; Bhanja, Aditi; Stark, Nicholas; Hardy, James; Peabody, Christopher R. (2022). How psychological safety and feeling heard relate to burnout and adaptation amid uncertainty. Health Care Management Review 47(4):p 308-316, 10/12 2022. DOI: 10.1097/HMR.0000000000000338

O'Donovan, Róisín & Mcauliffe, Eilish. (2020). A systematic review exploring the content and outcomes of interventions to improve psychological safety, speaking up and voice behaviour. BMC Health Services Research. 20. 10.1186/s12913-020-4931-2.

Sewell, Dave (2023, Jan 13).Why Psychological Safety Should Be Your Focus For 2023 And Beyond. https://www.brainzmagazine.com/post/why-psychological-safety-should-be-your- focus-for-2023-and-beyond

4

Effect of BBS on Safety Performance

Best BBS (behaviour based safety) observers when recognised by their company, tend to create more best observers. More observers, more observations, more spot-corrections of unsafe behaviours and barriers daily.

A study examined the effectiveness of BBS programme in improving safe behaviours and safety climate of organization. BBS programme was applied to the steel manufacturing and construction sites. The dependent variables were measured by the percentage of employees' safe behaviours observed and perceived safe behaviours and safety climate of employees. BBS programme consisted of goal-setting, feedback, and incentive. The one group pre-test-post-test design was adopted for perceived safe behaviours and safety climate. Observed safe behaviours were measured during the baseline and intervention phases (AB design). The results indicated that the mean percentage of employees' safe behaviours observed increased after introducing BBS programme. Also, the mean scores of perceived safe behaviours and safety climate of employees significantly increased (Moon *et al.*, 2012). Research and industry experience suggest that the more successful BBS processes create positive and collaborative effort to improve safety culture. The empirical basis for BBS continues to mature and provide guidance to both practitioners and companies (Spigener *et al.*, 2022).

Another study evaluated the construction of petrochemical plants and refineries. The 14 total projects evaluated was a mixture of six Greenfield and eight Brownfield projects. Although the data evaluated was only from Technip owned projects, the findings of this report may be valid for other companies as guidance in considering the implementation of a behaviour based safety programme on particular project or site location. The cards captured both positive and negative observations, however the data evaluated in this report includes the sum of all safe and unsafe observations for each month. This may be a limitation when evaluating the correlation between observations and first aid, since it will not capture the impact of safe vs unsafe observations. Since the basis of BBS is engaging all levels of the workforce, the overall goal is to improve safety culture. By improving safety culture, we typically expect to observe increased near-miss reporting and decreased number of injuries, or in this case first aid. To better optimise this study in the future, gauging the quality of each BBS observation submitted is critical to ensuring reliable data. This study was solely analyzing the observation numbers based on the total number of participants rather than evaluating each observation for quality. In this case, a good quality observation is one that involves a conversation by the observer to either correct an unsafe behaviour or reinforce a safe behaviour. The conversation has to also be well-received by the individual being observed to ensure the desired action is sustainable. As a further expansion of this study, it is recommended to design a mechanism to gauge the quality of the observations and conduct a separate analysis utilizing only the high quality observations (Fazilov *et al.*, 2018).

BBS approach is the usage of science for changing the behaviour of an individual. BBS focuses on action of workmen on day-to-day safety behaviour and its improvement. This study presented a case study within the multi-storey building construction in India. This research work outlined the BBS method into seven steps and encapsulated a number of behavioural safety methods to prevent the workplace accident. The objective of this paper was to create a safe work environment in construction industries by decreasing frequency severity of injuries and increase the safe behaviour. The outcome of this research work revealed that a method related to observation, a real-time measure of safety behaviour with appreciative and constructive feedback for the significant improvement of the safety performance in multi-storey building construction.

Observers were educated to provide appreciative feedback when the workers performed the task safely and to offer constructive feedback to unsafe task performers. Baseline data of current safety performance was calculated before the BBS approach implementation and compared with the safety performance weekly data to identify the improvements (Dinagaran *et al.*, 2020).

BBS has been widely implemented for more than 40 years to help improve safety performance and prevent serious injuries and fatalities (SIFs). There are several factors that have driven the popularity of BBS. More than half (52%) of occupational safety and health professionals in a 2017 survey by *Industrial Safety and Hygiene News* (*ISHN*) reported a major impact challenge was ensuring employee behavioural reliability in terms of consistent safe behaviours. In a 2015 ISHN survey, 54% of professionals said increasing employee engagement and participation was a top goal. BBS involves the use of behavioural checklists to note both safe and risky behaviours to provide employees immediate safety feedback. Observations based on checklists of key risks and the immediate feedback given to employees increase engagement and participation. And in the 2017

ISHN survey, 56% said building and maintaining a culture inclusive of safety and health values and interventions was a high priority, and 56% reported reducing SIFs to be a high priority. BBS, especially its more recent incarnations, such as so-called BBS 2.0, go beyond a strict focus on reducing injuries (and often unfortunately blaming the victim) to take a more holistic approach that focuses not only on behaviours, but work environment, cultural antecedents, systems and employee attitudes to strengthen organisational cultures, values and performance (Johnson, 2021).

The change in positive safety culture over the years and its sustainability need to be constantly explored. The management should continuously monitor and evaluate their strategies while delivering multifaceted interventions to be more specifically focused and to motivate workers to be enthusiastic in sustaining safety culture (Wong *et al.*, 2021).

Sembcorp Energy India Limited (SEIL) manages health, safety and environment (HSE) responsibility as its core value. To further strengthen the safety culture and secure a positive behavioural change within the workplace, SEIL has implemented and integrated BBS into its safety systems across all the assets. SEIL has a target to reduce unsafe behaviour in increments. SEIL believes that most of the safety incidents are caused due to unsafe behaviour. ISO 45001:2018 mandates that human competence and behavioural elements need to be considered in risk assessment and as an internal issue for managing risks. A BBS steering committee led by the Business Heads Thermal and Renewable BU's, including Plant Heads, Senior HODs and Safety Heads guides and monitors implementation of the BBS implementation action plan at SEIL. As part of BBS, unsafe behaviour are being spotted and corrected on the spot. Both safe and at-risk behaviours are tracked, analyzed and displayed (SEIL, 2023).

REFERENCES

Dinagaran, D.; Balasubramanian, K. R.; Sivapirakasam, S. P. (2020). Behaviour Based Safety Approach to Improve Workplace Safety in Multistory Building Construction. Advanced Science, Engineering and Medicine, Volume 12, Number 12, December 2020, pp. 1491-1499(9). DOI: https:// doi.org/10.1166/asem.2020.2588

Fazilov, Jamil & Senouci, Ahmed & Al-Derham, Hassan. (2018). Using Behavioural Based Safety to Enhance Safety Performance.

Journal of Civil Engineering and Construction. 7. 192. 10.32732/jcec.2018.7.4.192.

Johnson, Dave (2021, July 6).Breathing new life into Behaviour-Based Safety (BBS) programmes.https://www.ishn.com/articles/113027-breathing-new-life-into-behaviour-based-safety-bbs-programmes

Moon, Kwangsu & Lee, Kyehoon & Lee, Jaehee & Oah, Shezeen. (2012). The effect of behaviour based safety(BBS) programme on safety climate and safety behaviours. Korean Journal of Industrial and Organizational Psychology. 25. 349-372. 10.24230/kjiop.v25i2.349-372.

SEIL (2023). Behaviour Based Safety (BBS) Implemented at SEIL. https://www.sembcorpenergyindia.com/CSR/BBS

Spigener Jim, Gennifer Lyon & Terry McSween (2022). Behaviour-based safety 2022: today's evidence, Journal of Organizational Behaviour Management, 42:4, 336-359, DOI: 10.1080/01608061.2022.2048943

Wong SY, Fu ACL, Han J, Lin J, Lau MC. (2021). Effectiveness of customised safety intervention programmes to increase the safety culture of hospital staff. BMJ Open Qual. 2021 Oct; 10(4):e000962. doi: 10.1136/bmjoq-2020-000962. PMID: 34625426; PMCID: PMC8504354.

5

Risk Perceptions

Business risks are numerous, so hands and minds have to be innumerable to control them. How the businesses in this world are carried out amidst unending list of business risks such as safety, health, environment, political, climate, geographical, cyber, inflation, manpower, etc.? Hence, if employees, contractors, workmen and everyone else who joins hands to support the businesses in such scenarios, they make their own careers and life comfortable and easy to carry on for our own bread and butter and so on.

People think that risk is related to the use of chemicals, or electrical equipment and so on. But the risk is present in normal working or living conditions. Opening the door, while walking on the road, entering the lift, getting up from the bed. All these behaviours have resulted into serious incidents and injuries.

Whatever risks are assessed or identified, some risks remain unidentified, unknown or un-assessed which lead to incidents or accidents. Risk can be prevalent in any situation, known or unknown.

In order to define the risk to control it, regular internal risk assessment and correction on daily basis and by every employee and contract workmen rather than only auditors or HSE persons, become more important for risk control.

Boosting risk perceptions and letting everyone to control the risk is what is explained by ISO45001 by worker participation. Worker refers to a person performing work or work related activities under the management of the organization. That can be anybody: employees, trainees, contractors and freelancers. Similarly, workplace refers to the place where a person goes for work purposes – not just your office. A risk in ISO 45001 is defined as an effect of uncertainty. So while a hazard is the part of your process that could potentially affect workers' wellbeing, the risk is the likelihood that harm will occur. Worker's participation and consultation are sufficiently important in ISO 45001 to merit separate definitions.

Participation refers to the involvement in decision-making, consultation refers to seeking views before making a decision (Bureau Veritas, 2020).

Mobilising the entire workforce in an organisation is crucial to gain the workers' participation in risk identification and control. The methodology, guidance, reinforcement, roadmap and handholding are needed for moving the workers for participation. This is what is called an organisational long-term planned intervention for implementation of risk observations and correction in a timeframe which is the quickest before the risk can harm any one at site. In this regard, a behavioural science mentor's role is very important in reviewing the progress in terms of incremental mobilisation of workers into the risk perceptions and spot-corrections.

OHS is an important issue, since it has great impact on the cost, productivity, and social reputation of a company. Occupational hazards have attracted considerable attention from both researchers and practitioners, because they can cause financial and personal loss as well as intangible damage within organizations and enterprises worldwide. Our aim is to develop a new model to assess and rank the risk of occupational hazards and identify high-risk hazards for the promotion of occupational health. An extended evaluation based on distance from average solution (EDAS) method is introduced to determine the risk priorities of occupational hazards. Moreover, a combination weighting method is adopted to derive the relative weights of risk criteria. Hazards were determined as the most serious, i.e., collision with immobile objects or being struck by moving objects; fall of a person from height; and trapping, being crushed-inside or between objects (Liu *et al.*, 2021).

Work and workplaces are constantly changing with the introduction of new technologies, substances and work processes, changes in the structure of the workforce and the labour market, and new forms of employment and work organisation. This may give rise to new risks and challenges to workers' safety and health. These must be anticipated and addressed in order to ensure safe and healthy workplaces in the future. One of EU-OSHA's key objectives is the identification and provision of credible, high-quality data of these new and emerging occupational safety and health (OSH) risks that meet the needs of policy-makers and researchers and allow them to take timely and effective action. EU-OSHA's European Risk Observatory gathers and examines data, drawing on research and expert consultations, on trends and underlying factors having an impact on workplaces and workers' safety and health. It produces discussion papers, reports, summaries and visualisations targeted at policy-makers, social partners, researchers and workplace intermediaries at the EU and national level to provide them with the information and tools necessary to address the identified new and emerging challenges effectively. The ultimate aim is to raise awareness of how changes of all kinds — technological, societal, political and economical are likely to affect the safety and health of workers, as well to encourage timely prevention of future OSH challenges in order to ensure safe and healthy workplaces of tomorrow (EU-OSHA, 2023).

A global risk is the possibility of the occurrence of an event or condition which, if it occurs, would negatively impact a significant proportion of global GDP, population or natural resources. The Global Risks Perception Survey (GRPS) is the World Economic Forum's source of original risks data, harnessing the expertise of the Forum's extensive network of academic, business, government, civil society and thought leaders. The list of 32 global risks included cost of living crisis, misinformation and disinformation. Failure of climate-change adaption, and failure to mitigate climate change were added. Currently, manifesting risks included continued waves of COVID-19, cost of living crisis, cyber attacks on critical infrastructure, debt crisis, deployment of chemical and biological weapons on a catastrophic scale, deployment of nuclear weapons on a catastrophic scale, disruptions in global supply chains for non-food goods, energy supply crisis, failure to set and meet national net-zero targets, food supply crisis, rising inflation, structural failures in health systems, weakening of human rights, and weaponisation of economic policy (World Economic Forum, 2023).

REFERENCES

Bureau Veritas (2020, Aug 20).ISO 45001 TERMS AND DEFINITIONS: WHAT'S NEW IN CLAUSE 3? https://certification.bureauveritas.com/magazine/iso-45001-terms-and-definitions-whats- new-clause-3

EU-OSHA (2023). Emerging risks. https://osha.europa.eu/en/emerging-risks

Liu, Ran & Mou, Xun & Liu, Hu-Chen. (2021). New Model for Occupational Health and Safety Risk Assessment based on Combination Weighting and Uncertain Linguistic Information. IISE Transactions on Occupational Ergonomics and Human Factors. 8. 1-21.

10.1080/24725838.2021.1875519.

World Economic Forum (2023, January 11) Global Risks Report 2023. https://www.weforum.org/reports/global-risks-report-2023/in-full/appendix-a-technical-notes- global-risks-perception-survey-2022-2023

6

To Be a Global Company with Positive Safety Culture

When safety is relegated to a check-the-box exercise, companies are more likely to experience stagnant or incremental safety improvements. Organizations that approach safety as a cultural value and a commitment to their people and their work can promote meaningful change that everyone across the organization can and should be a part of. To embed safety in the corporate culture, companies must engage stakeholders across the board, from employees to executive leadership, through open dialogue (Boutetière *et al.*, 2019).

The new equation is turning resources into resourceful. Companies that promote a culture of health, safety, and wellbeing outperform in the marketplace. Employers, fund managers, and fund investors would be well served by including strategies that assess a company's commitment to the health, safety, and wellbeing of their workforce when evaluating investments in their enterprises and portfolios. There is a growing body of evidence that supports the concept that a healthy workforce provides a competitive business advantage. Unhealthy and unsafe employees spend more on healthcare, and unsafe behaviour is a direct cost for most large and mid-sized employers. Even more costly are the losses in productivity, an estimated $2 to $3 additional dollars for each dollar spent on direct healthcare costs.

Moreover, companies that focus on health and safety for their workforce may create a culture that supports a healthy workforce and increases the percentage of employees engaged and committed to the organization's success (Raymond and Phares, 2021).

Companies before becoming a global entity, need to understand first that a positive safety culture is all about implementing a consciousness among the workers about the sense of brotherhood, affection, affiliation, support and spot-correction of behaviours and barriers.

We need to differentiate between the fake and ground level safety cultures. Fake safety culture find place only in documents for gaining safety awards or business certifications, not visible in ground reality. Real-time safety culture refers to company procedures that reinforce every day involvement of everyone in contributing for positive safety culture at sites, offices and everywhere, in personal life as well.

Management's thought process to be a global company with positive safety culture, is an emerging scenario that can pave the way for business excellence. But the caution here is that any safety culture approach when not integrated with the company's policy and performance falls apart after some time. So beware that this organisational cognitive error is avoided.

Macro aspects of safety culture such as management's sincere speeches, displays, certifications are for business perspective, but if micro aspects of positive safety culture such as daily safety conversations between frontline engineers, supervisors, workers are not meaningful for creating safe work, the balance between the micro and macro aspects do not fit well. The gap exists and it becomes complex to sort out issues for anybody at workplace, for which consequences are only incidents and related pains.

Safety leadership is a business perspective. Strong businesses are shaped by their culture. Creating a safe production culture improves operations and is reflected positively in profit margins, as demonstrated by Paul O'Neill's work as CEO of Alcoa. Now more than ever, putting safety first when it comes to production is essential. This necessity is being recognized by business and safety leaders. Throughout the pandemic, many companies stepped up to the challenge and made huge leaps in workplace safety leadership in an accelerated timeframe. In fact, I spoke to one leader who said his organization made six years' worth of progress in safety leadership in just six weeks as a result of their leadership focus (Michrowski, 2021).

Moving from a safety policy to a safety culture requires guidelines that are aligned with the organizational brand, mission statement, principles, and values. Cultivating positive safety culture is becoming a top priority for many businesses because safety matters to employees and the bottom line. A company with a strong safety culture will have a commitment to safety from both leadership and workers. Companies that can convey care, compassion, and a desire for everyone to go home safe at night will have a better response than those that solely deliver a message of restrictions or punishment for missing the target mark (SSOE, 2021).

A proactive safety culture goes together with the company's corporate culture and values. Every year, nearly 3 million people die due to exposure to common risk factors in the workplace. Work related diseases were responsible for 81 per cent of all work related deaths in 2016, with an estimated 745,000 deaths attributed to diseases caused by long working hours. Since the 1980s, the world has recognized Workers' Memorial Day, which honours those workers killed, injured or disabled on the job. Since 2003, the International Labour Organization (ILO) has been commemorating the World Day for Safety and Health at Work annually on 28 April, promoting good practices for occupational safety and health (OSH) and shedding light on key related issues (United Nations, 2022).

Companies with a strong safety culture invest in creating lines of open communication throughout their organisation. Installing a positive safety culture within the workplace improves employees' safety and impacts how employees feel about their company, increasing the positive feelings about their organisation (Buzinkay, 2023).

For best possible protection of employees, technical and organizational occupational safety must be supplemented by a behaviour component, precisely called corporate safety culture, often referred to as behaviour based safety (BBS). BBS encourages employees to think proactively and motivates them to take care of both themselves and their colleagues. A team spirit emerges that motivates each individual to take accountability for safety standards and to help prevent accidents. This process moves the organization closer to vision zero harm, resulting in a sustainable safety culture (TÜV Rheinland, 2023).

REFERENCES

Boutetière Hortense de la, Rose Julie, and Spinoy Bernadette (2019, July 17). Transforming safety culture: Insights from the trenches at a leading oil and gas company. https:// www.mckinsey.com/capabilities/people-and-organizational-performance/our-insights/transforming-safety-culture-insights-from-the-trenches-at-a-leading-oil-and-gas-company

Buzinkay, Mark (2023, January12). Underground Mining Safety: ImplementingA Positive Safety Culture. https://www.identecsolutions.com/news/underground-mining-safety-implementing- a-positive-safety-culture

Michrowski, Eric (2021, Dec 1). Beyond Back To Normal: Embedding Positive Changes Into Your Safety Culture.https://www.forbes.com/sites/forbesbusinesscouncil/2021/12/01/beyond- back-to-normal-embedding-positive-changes-into-your-safety-culture/?sh=702585e932e9

Raymond, Fabius, and Phares, Sharon (2021). Companies That Promote a Culture of Health, Safety, and Wellbeing Outperform in the Marketplace. Journal of Occupational and Environmental Medicine 63(6):p 456-461, June 2021. | DOI: 10.1097/JOM.0000000000002153

SSOE (2021, November 1). Creating a Positive Safety Culture. https://www.ssoe.com/creating-a-positive-safety-culture-2/

TÜV Rheinland (2023). Safety culture & behaviour based safety– the power of habits. https://www.tuv.com/united-kingdom/en/lp/safety-culture/main-navigation/safety-culture/

United Nations (2022, April 28). Together We Can Build a Culture of Safety and Health at Work. https://www.un.org/en/un-chronicle/together-we-can-build-culture-safety-and- health-work

7

Resilient Organisations and Positive Safety Culture

Developing resilient organisations and positive safety culture would mean to raise own implementation experience, data and information within the organisation so that it can bounce forward in case of incidents, failure or uncertainty. The development of a positive safety culture and constructive attitudes towards safety is typically presented as an important and effective proactive strategy to promote and maintain a safe workplace. Safety culture is related with organizational resilience in a variety of ways. However, several cultural facets appear to be associated with the ability to adapt to change and disturbance, namely, interpersonal relationships at work and the involvement of workers and the traditional conflict between productivity and safety (D'Oliveira & Mário, 2010).

Dysfunctional cultures can lead to disregard for safety. Challenging times put company's culture to the test. Leader's decisions are scrutinized. Employees immediately judge whether actions are in alignment with the values of the organization. Ten years of positive culture can dissolve overnight when crisis hit. People can also lose trust in leaders when decisions take longer than expected, don't take into consideration all valued stakeholders, and don't come from a value system of compassion and support. Members of resilient teams collectively believe they can effectively complete tasks together. There are three factors you can readily influence to improve a team's actual and perceived execution efficacy. Team members are in roles that are an excellent fit with their innate strengths, skills, and abilities. Team members cooperate well in accomplishing the team's goals. Decision-making speed: decisions are made in a timely manner (Wastag, 2020).

As a CEO, it is easy to declare the intent of having a strong and resilient safety culture at town halls, in management meetings, and in weekly reports to the field. It is another thing to act on it to building a strong and resilient safety culture. Many of those leaders are stuck, not sure how to build a strong and resilient safety culture within their organization (Davey, 2021).

Resilience is required for businesses to respond to disruptions as well as adapt to challenging conditions, leveraging opportunities and delivering sustainable performance improvement. Senior executives need to both insure against bad events, while at the same time adapt before the cost of not doing so becomes too great. Identifying best practices in organisational resilience is a significant challenge. As Howard Kerr, chief executive of BSI, says: "Striving for excellence requires business leaders to challenge complacency, promote vigilance and embrace the need for continual improvement. Many organisations are sleepwalking to disaster, waiting out a storm, is no longer an option, rather move forward to positive safety culture and build resilience (SHEQ, 2021).

Resilience in positive psychology refers to the ability to cope with whatever life throws at you. Resilient people are knocked down by challenges, but they return stronger and more steadfast than before (Malik, 2021). The companies that focus on building resilient operations, teams, and leaders would invest in culture now and for the future. Raising the resilience of your organization would necessitate a safety culture that fosters safe practices. Resilient organizations don't just bounce back from misfortune or change; they bounce forward. They absorb the shocks and turn them into opportunities to capture sustainable, inclusive growth. When challenges emerge, leaders and teams in resilient organizations quickly assess the situation, reorient themselves, double down on what's working, and walk away from what's not (Maor, *et al.*, 2022). Positive changes are the pulse of resilient culture.

The increasing injury and fatality rate implies that conventional safety culture is unable to match the increasing safety requirement of industry. One promising approach is establishing resilience safety culture for the industry which performs better in complying with real situations and considering sufficiently necessary dimensions and relationships. However, it is a bit hard to easily and fully understand without the implementation roadmap (Haihui, 2022).

An organisation that is resilient simply applies and improves long-term positive safety culture of trust and ensuring good health, safety, and wellbeing of workers.

Resilient organizations make psychological safety a strategic priority. The simple business case for each dimension of resilience is well known. Ethical business behaviour (integrity) enhances financial performance, employees who generate and share more ideas improve profitability through innovation, and organizational diversity predicts higher financial returns (inclusion). Both integrity and inclusion are key elements of assessing an organization's ESG (environment, sustainability, and governance) commitments and performance. Beyond their direct impacts on the bottom line, these three dimensions share an intrinsic connection. Psychological safety is at their core, and any breach erodes their foundation. The fear of retaliation for speaking up compromises integrity, curbing creative ideation leads to stagnation, and disrespectful interactions have a disproportionately toxic impact on engagement and belonging (Gube and Hennelly, 2022).

Resilience is both a highly interrelated construct on the individual and organizational level and also positively linked to perceptions of transformation as an indicator for demonstration of resilience, and efficacy as a full mediation on the team level (Gröschke *et al.*, 2022). The concept of resilient safety culture reflects and explains how an organisation's psychological, behavioural, and contextual capabilities can be used to anticipate, monitor, respond, and learn in order to better manage safety risks. Having a resilient safety culture means continuously improving processes by committed staff who systematically cope with the complexity and unpredictability of today's business environment (MDPI, 2023).

REFERENCES

Davey, Tyler (2021, July 14). Building a Strong and Resilient Safety Culture Starts with the C- Suite. https://www.safeopedia.com/building-a-strong-and-resilient-safety-culture-starts- with-the-c-suite/2/8991

D'Oliveira, Teresa & Mário, Cláudia. (2010, Sept). Organizational safety: From safety culture to organizational resilience. Conference: 29th Conference of the European Association for Aviation Psychology. https://www.researchgate.net/publication/
267926244_Organizational_safety_From_safety_culture_to_organizational_resilience

Gube Maren and Hennelly Debra Sabatini (2022, August 25).Resilient Organizations Make Psychological Safety a Strategic Priority. https://hbr.org/2022/08/resilient-organizations- make-psychological-safety-a-strategic-priority

Gröschke D, Hofmann E, Müller ND, Wolf J. (2022). Individual and organizational resilience- Insights from healthcare providers in Germany during the COVID-19 pandemic. Front Psychol. 2022 Aug 25;13:965380. doi: 10.3389/fpsyg.2022.965380. PMID: 36092080; PMCID: PMC9453859.

Haihui Yao (2022). A model for establishing resilience safety culture for the construction industry, International Journal of Occupational Safety and Ergonomics, DOI: 10.1080/10803548.2022.2089468

Malik, Sonia (2021). Building Organizational Resilience with a Highly Skilled Learner Ecosystem. https://trainingindustry.com/magazine/may-jun-2021/building-organizational- resilience-with-a-highly-skilled-learner-ecosystem/

Maor Dana, Michael Park, and Brooke Weddle (2022, Oct 12). Raising the resilience of your organisation. https://www.mckinsey.com/

capabilities/people-and-organizational-performance/our-insights/raising-the-resilience-of-your-organization MDPI (2023). Special Issue Resilient Safety Culture. https://www.mdpi.com/journal/safety/special_issues/resilient_safety_culture

SHEQ (2021, Jan 11). Is Your Organisation Resilient? Https://Sheqmanagement.Com/Is-Your- Organisation-Resilient/Wastag, Alice (2020, April 28). Culture at Work: Three Signs of a Resilient Organization. https://www.glintinc.com/blog/culture-at-work-three-signs-of-a-resilient-organization/

8

Managements Prioritise on the Safety Culture Drive

Every employee/worker ought to prioritise on saving human life, make time for an observation round at site daily, without fail, look for at-risk behaviour to spot-correct in a positive way. Any truly successful company culture that focuses on safety performance depends on leaders who are committed to prioritizing safety in everyday transactions.

Most organisations conduct safety drama and lip service, without adequate budget for developing safety culture for their businesses. If managers at all levels are not seen participating in safety tours or inspections, it sends the message that safety is not a priority. There are three important aspects of the safety culture. The psychological aspect, which refers to how employees feel about safety and the safety management system. The behavioural aspect, which refers to what employees do within the organisation. The situational aspect, which refers to the organisation's policies, procedures, and ways by which it achieves its objectives. These three aspects are interrelated and they define the safety culture of the organisation (Oladotun, 2021).

Risk has a definition to the extent of our awareness, what if all employees are aware of the risk and its control on the spot, then it becomes an organisational safety culture, which every company management needs to be aware of, prioritise for, implement it, review and go on.

Capitalize on a strong safety culture. As a CEO, you'll want to prioritize both the safety and wellbeing of your employees and the profitability of your company. The key to securing both is avoiding losses, and one way to achieve that is by building a strong safety culture. To create a robust organizational culture, it is crucial to ensure that safety policies and procedures are used to both identify and address potential issues. A culture based safety strategy will also demonstrate a commitment to safety towards employees, investors and customers alike, and can be used to track the success of safety initiatives. Personally, as well as occupationally, turning a blind eye to risk is a very expensive habit (Torkel, 2023). I lost my sister-in-law in mobility from one hospital to another, also I lost my sister in mobility from house to hospital, both were critically ill, these are two extremely unsafe behaviours, that had happened being unaware of the consequences, which could be avoided. Never be blind to risk, it is expensive beyond one's imagination.

When employees feel safe at work, they are happier and perform better. Therefore, business leaders must prioritize creating a safe culture. Safety culture in the workplace is worth the investment, giving you and your employees a morale boost by fostering a sense of security (Catsavis, 2022). Safety culture suffers from the management's empty promises and speeches.

Improving safety culture is a long organisational process. There are top three priorities for EHS professionals in 2023. Standardizing

EHS practices, improve analysis capabilities and eliminate manual forms/digitize processes. Standardizing EHS practices at large corporations with multiple locations across different states or countries is challenging. This issue becomes more complicated when safety teams are small and can only visit a site once or twice a year. In addition, recently acquired locations may have their own safety and health processes that have evolved organically over the years. Improving EHS analysis capabilities would mean that some of the data processes may be on paper in a file cabinet, others in an Excel sheet, and some in a more modern form of EHS software. Valuable information is lost because they are separated and do not communicate. As a result, companies lose the ability to analyze their safety data and miss an excellent opportunity to gain deeper insight into their organization and stop an accident or non-compliance before it happens. Analysis capabilities help uncover variations and risks and make standardization of EHS processes and policies more effective. Digitizing EHS means that valuable data is available to stakeholders immediately. Take an accident or injury witness statement, for example. Management traditionally would need to call supervisors and ask for that information or wait for the paper document to be scanned and emailed to them. With digital forms, that witness statement is available immediately to everybody who needs it. By eliminating these delays in reporting, companies can respond to root causes, non-compliance, and workplace hazards immediately (ProcessMAP, 2022).

CEO challenges the leaders about their daily visible efforts on building positive safety culture. "My personal journey began in the army when I first observed the best leaders prioritize the welfare of the troops in their command. Leading the exercise, checking on the wellbeing of the soldiers and taking care of themselves only after everyone else was accounted for, was ingrained in my memory. The visual has stuck with me throughout my career. I try to make sure everyone at STACK is prioritized before I worry about me. We live in such a dynamic time that it must start with the wellbeing of our employees. If we do not, at a minimum, prioritize human life in physical safety and mental health, I am not sure the rest of it matters". Early in STACK's growth, we recognized the inherent risks to workers in the construction trades and empathized with the challenges faced daily by the tradesmen and women. Although these workers are not direct employees of STACK, they are our partners, and they have people in their lives who count on them to come home safely. It is part of our ethical culture and CSR to value these partners and do our part to ensure that they are safe to construct our projects. We can delegate the authority to help with a project to our contractor partners, but the responsibility for safety at all levels rests with the CEO. Under Cox's leadership, STACK brings a safety-first perspective to every aspect of the design, construction and critical operations of its data centres. Cox has increased the EHS team to nearly a dozen full-time safety employees, along with additional safety consultants, in the past year. In less than a year, each one of the company's construction projects has been staffed with a full-time STACK safety representative. He consistently challenges the team to know senior leaders from the company's general contractors and vendor partners to ensure they have a deep respect for safety, and work with them to improve their EHS practices (Safety+ Health, 2023).

REFERENCES

Catsavis, Lindsay (2022, April 28). How to Improve Safety Culture in the Workplace and the Company & Employee Benefits of Doing So. https://www.supplychain247.com/article/ how_to_improve_safety_culture_in_the_workplace_and_the_benefits_of_doing_so

Oladotun A. (2021, Jun 8). Managing Organisation Safety Culture. https://www.linkedin.com/pulse/managing-organisation-safety-culture-oladotun-akanji

ProcessMAP (2022). What Are The Top Three Priorities For EHS Professionals In 2023 And Why? https://www.processmap.com/ehs-software/what-are-the-top-three-priorities-for-ehs- professionals-in-2023-and-why/Safety+ Health (2023, January 29). The 2023 CEOs Who "Get It". https://www.safetyandhealthmagazine.com/articles/23407-2023-ceos-who-get-it?page=4

Torkel, Soma (2023, February, 13). Capitalize on a Strong Safety Culture. https://sayfr.com/insights/capitalize-on-a-strong-safety-culture

9

Passion for Safety Culture Transformation

How many managing directors review their company's safety culture every month or quarter? Is it necessary?

If leaders are passionate, they can achieve safety culture transformation for their companies.

How sincerely one talks about safety culture, reflects his own introduction as well as of his company he works for.

Safety culture is the way, safety is perceived, valued and prioritised in an organisation. To change unsafe behaviour for a safe mindset, it requires consistency and passion.

Having a passion for safety means actively caring about your people and your operations. If you take care of your people, they will be more productive.

How do company directors support safety culture excellence is a deep question to explore the goal of incidents-free status? The top/site management at large are responsible for weak safety culture at the corporates as well as sites resulting in incidents and fatalities. Almost 80% industry professionals observed lack of management's will to support the safety culture, which amounts to a lag in business sustainability. Top managements need guidance about interventions leading to safety culture transformation (Kaila, 2022).

How many managing directors in India review their company's safety culture every month or quarter? Is it necessary?

Nearly 102 industry leaders responded:

1. Vasudha Pharma and Gharda Chemicals: Need to implement safety culture in every industry. It is much necessary to review safety culture every month and every MD should do it on priority.
2. A safety professional: Focus on HSE will make a big difference. In every VP and GM meeting, initiation should be only on HSE. Any failure or incident in his area will reduce 50% of his bonus in a year.
3. Navin Flourine: I think only those companies who have implemented BBS, or may be MNC's safety culture is reviewed by their top leaders. There is no compulsion or mandate under regulations for managing directors (MD) to review their company's safety culture.
4. Maheshwaran, a safety professional: I have moved to Abu Dhabi for an assignment with one of the power and desalination plant. I am reporting to my MD. He is focused on safety a lot. He participates in 3 safety inspections every week. He brings in lot of motivation in all employees by wearing reflective coverall always.
5. A safety professional: I have seen this practice in Nerolac Paint but frequency is once in a two year.
6. Indeed it is necessary, however good companies give due importance, many companies do lip service of giving importance, and a large number of MSMEs need to learn a lot in this area.

7. A safety professional: Very few indian companies do this, may be 10%. But most of the MNCs having their top heads reviewing safety culture, it is very much necessary.
8. I think not more than 5% of the MDs review safety culture that too as a part of compliance obligation. It is very much necessary as it is safety and it is always top driven. For ONGC: may be 20%. There is Board above MD. Board include independent Directors also. Board has sub-committees also. One such sub-committee is on HSE. That meets every quarter. But that also does not discuss safety culture on regular basis. It is in ONGC and other PSUs.
9. According to a retired Director of Factories, quite a few, MD's review at this periodicity. They can be counted on finger tips. Rest gets lighted up only when some mishap occurs. Necessity cannot be ruled out.
10. AFCONS: Very few are showing concern. It is very much essential and it sends the message down the line.
11. Sembcorp does every month. Important thing is that MD must listen to subject matter expert in their team because they live safety on daily basis.
12. IOCL: MD reviews only when emergency arises and before Annual Board Meeting (to face stakeholders). It is necessary to review of safety culture to assess the position of safety culture indicators whether improving or falling down.
13. OPAL: It should be done. But I think only 5% of the managing directors may be doing.
14. A safety professional: It is purely an essential management tool as part of the HSE system.
15. Torrent: Now in most of the big companies, MD reviews monthly and quarterly review by Board of Directors.
16. DCM Shriram: There are means and ways of reviews - sometimes formal and quite often informal, receiving updates from senior leadership team.

17. In many pharmaceutical and speciality chemical companies, MD & CEO review safety journey progress every month, some call HSE meet quarterly and some review annually.

The above data reveal that most managing directors in small, medium, or even large companies do not review safety culture, except a few multinational, public sector, or large companies, sometimes monthly, quarterly or annual basis, in a structured or an informal manner. This determines the motivation of employees or the company safety performance.

The spiritual, harmonious and passionate leadership that praises employees' achievements will encourage employees' hope and belief in the achievement of their goals, building their confidence and enthusiasm when engaging in safety work. Not only do individuals begin to work exceptionally, they also actively exhibit safety participation behaviours such as mutual assistance among colleagues, participate in safety promotion planning, and enhance workplace safety (Ali *et al.*, 2020). Spiritual leadership significantly improved employee safety performance (Liu, *et al.*, 2022).

Zafar (2022) defined responsibilities of the Managing Directors/ Chief Executives as below. They are responsible and accountable for health and safety performance at the organization; develop a strong, positive health and safety culture throughout the company and communicate it to all managers. This should ensure that all managers have a clear understanding of their health and safety responsibilities.

- Provide guidance and leadership on health and safety matters to their management team.
- Establish maximum health and safety standards within the organization.
- Ensure that adequate resources are available for the health and safety requirements within the organization and authorize any necessary major health and safety expenditures.
- Evaluate, approve and authorize health and safety-related projects developed by the organization's health and safety advisers.
- Review and approve health and safety policies, procedures, and programmes developed by the organization's managers.

- Ensure that working knowledge of the areas of health and safety that are regulated by various governmental agencies, particularly the HSE, local authorities, and the environment agency, are maintained.
- Ensure that health and safety is included as an agenda at all formal senior management meetings.
- Review and act upon major recommendations submitted by outside loss prevention consultants and insurance companies.
- Ensure that health and safety is included in any tours such as fire inspections of the organization's sites and note any observed acts or conditions that fall short of or exceed agreed health and safety standards.
- Ensure that all fatalities, major property losses, lost workdays injuries, and dangerous occurrences are investigated.
- Establish, implement and maintain a formal, written health and safety programme for the organization that encompasses all areas of significant health and safety risk.
- Appoint controls to ensure uniform adherence to the health and safety programme across the organization. These controls should include both corrective and follow-up actions.
- Attend the health and safety committee meetings at the organization.
- Review regularly, all health and safety activity reports and performance statistics.
- Review health and safety reports submitted by outside agencies and determine that any agreed actions have been taken.
- Review annually the effectiveness of the site health and safety programme.
- Appraise the performance of the health and safety advisers and provide guidance or training where necessary.
- Monitor the progress of managers and others towards achieving their health and safety objectives.
- Above all, the Managing Directors/Chief Executives should review the positive safety culture development for their businesses every month, and for safety meeting with the contract partners.

REFERENCES

Ali, Moazzam & Aziz, Shahzad & Pham, Nhat Tan & Babalola, Mayowa & Usman, Muhammad. (2020). A Positive Human Health Perspective on How Spiritual Leadership Weaves its Influence on Employee Safety Performance: The Role of Harmonious Safety Passion. Safety Science. (131). 10.1016/j.ssci.2020.104923.

Kaila, Harbans Lal (2020). Top Management's Will To Support Safety Culture. International Journal of Research - GRANTHAALAYAH, Vol. 10 No. 4 (2022): Volume 10 Issue 4 : April 2022. DOI: https://doi.org/10.29121/granthaalayah.v10.i4.2022.4573

Liu, Yuanyuan & Liu, Yunshuo & Liu, Pingqing & Liu, Dongxu & Liu, Shuzhen. (2022). The Spiritual Force of Safety: Effect of Spiritual Leadership on Employees' Safety Performance. International Journal of Occupational Safety and Ergonomics. 1-22. 10.1080/10803548.2022.2056379.

Zafar Shehzad (2022, March 25). Health And Safety Responsibilities Of Managing Directors/ Chief Executives. https://www.hseblog.com/health-and-safety-responsibilities-of-managing- directors-chief-executives/

10

A Case on Positive Safety Culture

Behaviour based safety or big brother safety (BBS) provides the necessary components of care and timely intervention. However needs to be backed up by a robust safety management system.

Review of BBS Data

At Hindalco Renukoot, BBS has been reported by employees on Enablon Portal. Each employee has target of at least 4 BBSO/ month as per schedule, which is further changeable based on place of observation.

BBS observation reported under 7 categories of PPE, position of people, reaction of people, tools & equipment, orderliness, procedures and safe-unsafe condition.

These safety contacts are being categorized in 5 categories, if found unsafe behaviour based on severity. 1 being lowest severity of first aid case and 5 being highest of fatal potential.

Observation is then reported to Department Head for Action Plan and closing.

All these observations of higher impacts have been discussed in steering committee for their closure status and re-discussion with department heads. Further opened critical BBS observations are discussed in Apex Meeting which is headed by Unit Head.

Observations concerned with specific Safety Agenda are shared with their respective task forces (TFs) such as Hot Work TF, Work at Height TF, Molten Metal TF, Road Safety TF, Gas Cylinder TF, Material handling TF, Electrical Safety TF, etc.

All other safety contacts by each observer are accessible to every employee for his understanding. Employees' BBS status for the month is communicated to all employees of each plant on the weekly basis.

Efficacy of BBS Implementation

BBS implementation has helped in bringing down the unsafe practices and behaviours across various safety standards such as work at height, hot work, electrical safety, operational discipline, confined spaces, etc.

It gives essence of recording safety observations apart from traditional safety approach which was mostly inclined towards PPE, tools-equipment conditions and SOP only. BBS enhances the observations and its corrections across various categories by monitoring reaction of people, position of people, orderliness level.

Comparative Summary of BBS Efficacy

Month	% of Safe behaviours	% of corrections
April 2021	78%	94.5
May 2021	85%	95.8

June 2021	84%	95.1
July 2021	90%	95.5
August 2021	92%	96
September 2021	91%	94.1
October 2021	89%	96
November 2021	93%	97.6
December 2021	90%	97.9
January 2022	93%	96.8
February 2022	94%	96.3
March 2022	93%	94.8

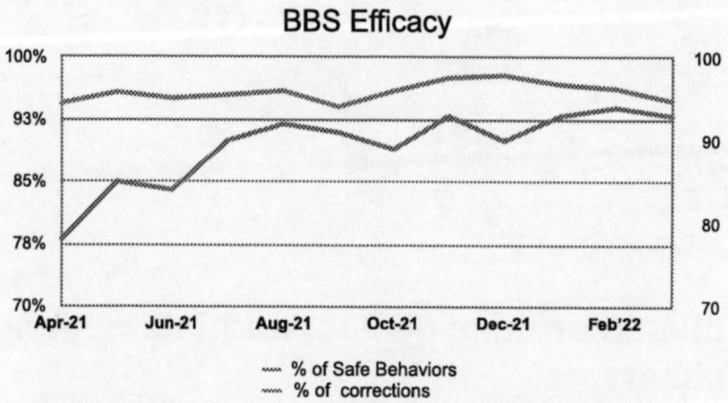

BBS banners display at work areas

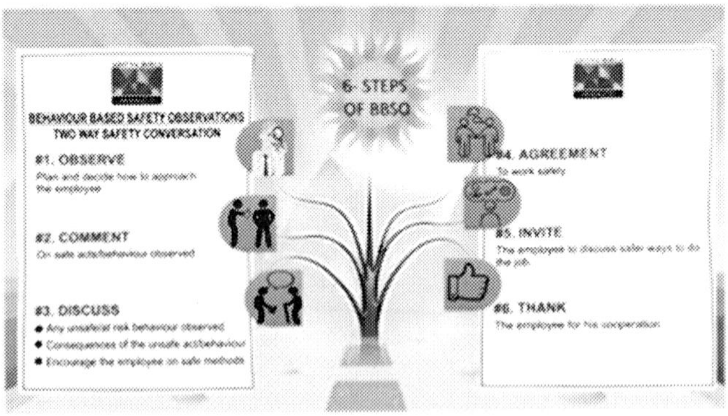

Visit by senior management and interactions with BBS observers

Senior management and interactions with BBS observers are held on regular basis to bring about safety culture in the unit. Leadership team holds interaction meetings in apex safety meetings, task force and BBS safety sub-committee meetings which are held every month.

Allocation of observers in different areas shift-wise

200 areas covered of plant including lesser visited area and remote area. Apart from schedules, observer can report instant BBSO any time for any locations.

Award/reward system for best observers:

Best BBS Award to 30 individuals quarterly and rolling trophy to one department of plant

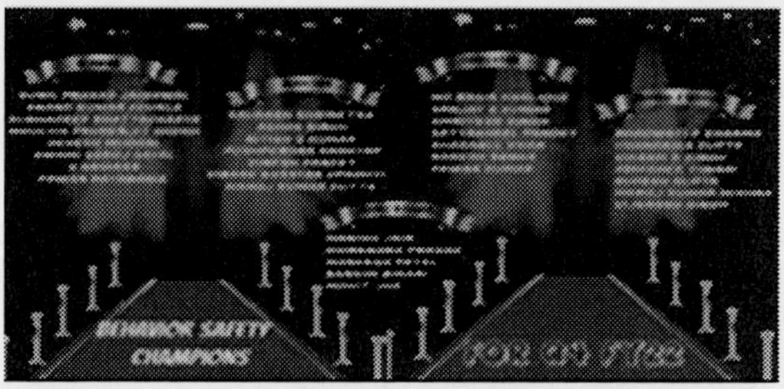

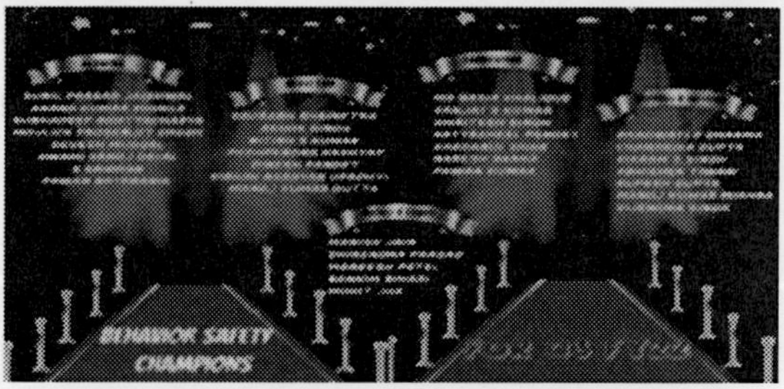

Effective participation and involvement of workers and other non-management staff of the Industry in the BBS implementation

Workers and associate supervisors do intervene on unsafe behaviour and report their BBS observations on hard copy. They too follow 6-step techniques for BBS and understanding it, as an act of promoting safe culture.

Innovational techniques used by the industry for BBS implementation

- Readily available QR code for scanning and ease in reporting of Behaviour Safety Observation.
- Inter-plant competition based on detailed KPI's
- Mentor-Mentee Programme for consistency in quality of BBSO reported.
- Observing BBS as Safety Theme of the Month
- Safety professionals audit observations
- Safety alerts to employees

Importance of BBS is enhancing the safe culture at your industry and the problems and hurdles faced by the industry in BBS implementation

At Hindalco Industries Ltd. Renukoot, BBS is considered the most fundamental and most important safety approach. BBS is at the core of each accident/incident investigation and unsafe behaviour has been informed to all safety forums of unit. Further BBS is at the center of all safety task forces. BBS steering committee co-ordinates with all other task forces in enhancing the safety culture at the unit. We had undertaken various activities like audits/inspections, preparation based on checklist and past experience, formation of teams, observing BBS as safety theme of the month to enhance the safety culture.

Many of our people are trained on "six steps" of BBS observation process and they are expected to use this process for behaviour based safety observations. However, in case some are not yet, they are encouraged at least to do "safety intervention" when they see any unsafe act, condition, practice or process. We encourage people to *"Say something when they see something is wrong or unsafe"* and accept their suggestion positively. It is now the duty of each one among us to stop unsafe act or practice or risk taken by people so that no one has to say….. I could have saved a life that day.

Future action plan for full implementation of BBS

Currently, BBS has been practised with all permanent and temporary employees working at unit including those who have been at non-plant activities such as: Admin, Commercial, Finance, IT, etc. Future plan is to extend the reporting of BBS observations, even by contractors on our Enablon Portal.

Review of the BBS processes checklist for your site as below.

Mark each process below out of 10. Check, what's lacking.

1.	Safety cultural shift from reactive, dependent culture to independent, interdependent culture	9
2.	Leadership increased involvement	10
3.	Monthly BBS meetings	10
4.	Incidents reduction	8
5.	Behavioural trends improvement	9
6.	Sharing of at-risk behaviours during TBT	10
7.	Motivational reward, recognition for observers, units	10
8.	Managements regular observation rounds	10
9.	Regular repeat BBS awareness sessions for spot-correction	9
10.	Quarterly reviews across units/sites	10

Total: $10 \times 10 = 100$

Your score: 95

11

Safety Culture Suffers from Disconnect and Decision Making

Globally, positive safety culture switch trends are encouraging industry more than ever before, coming together on it, is crucial for all stakeholders. At the same time, there is a disconnect between hierarchy groups in every organisation down the levels between management and non-management, contractors, workmen and so on. People carry their positions and speak with inflated ego. Hence, they do not open up or feel psychologically safe with each other.

For risk-based decision making, the frontline workers are critical layers of protection, as they are familiar with the organization's activities, equipment, and processes and the risks. Leveraging the day-to-day operational knowledge of personnel on the shop floor or in the field is key to success in any cultural transformation. As part of their ongoing ambition to become an incident-free organization, Tata Steel had already embarked on a holistic risk management and cultural transformation journey across all of its operations. When the new location was opened, mature safety procedures and best practices were adopted from their existing facilities in India and abroad. However, it became apparent that a large portion of the workers were contractors, a group that can be difficult for a company to directly influence. But Tata Steel doesn't differentiate between employees and contractors on the shop floor. Anyone who works in their facilities has the same expectations and responsibilities. Contractors are often considered 'outside folks', not company's employees. But an ideal and sustainable safety culture considers contractual employees as 'own employees' with respect to safety. We strongly believe in it and strive to involve our critical mass, including contractors, in our transformation journey (Tata Steel, 2021).

It is important to discern an impact of organization decision-making styles and safety accountability on occupational health and safety implementation. Nobody in an organisation takes commitment for decisions, though they all need and want a change. Every senior person takes approval from his higher bosses. For example, a HSE professional in a company, needs approval from his regional head, who needs consent of his directors. Thus, the first meeting for fixing positive safety culture takes place with the HSE professional and his team, then another second meeting with the regional head and his team, and third meeting with the directors' team. Hence, all the three meetings prolong the process of safety culture decision making. An effective OHS Implementation provides better control over OHS challenges. Implementation styles (rational and incremental) and safety accountability positively impact OHS implementation. OHS implementation should not be viewed as a social or technical issue alone. Strategic arrangements should be made at the organizational level to gain better control over OHS challenges by considering the institutional environment in which the organization operates (Nadeem *et al.*, 2022).

Even multi-nationals or pubic sector large organisations suffer from delaying or not taking decisions about safety culture transformation. The issues of corporate disconnect and decision making flow across the organisation, so much so that no one takes decisions, and remains disconnected over the years till such time that several incidents take place and till the initiative of positive safety culture is taken up and implemented further for an organisational change. However, for many companies, safety culture training is more important than its implementation due to lack of decision making, overlapping priorities, lack of perspectives, budgeting, management will and so on. A research proposed a methodology for risk-aware decision making related to the investment in safety. The methodology consisted of probabilistic risk assessment and following cost-benefit analysis for computing the risk for various safety regimes, which included individual as well as societal risk values, related to fatalities or serious injuries (Krasuski *et al.*, 2022).

Hutchinson (2022) discussed that even in dynamic and ill-structured situations, experienced decision makers can still quickly recognise and respond to situations; termed naturalistic decision making (NDM). One type of frame for decision making is termed the classical view. This sees decision making as people weighing up the pros and cons of different options. It is said to have little applicability to the dynamic and often rapidly changing situations facing people in complex and safety-critical industries. In these situations, NDM and recognition-primed decision making describe how people make decisions when facing ill-structured situations; shifting, ill-defined, or competing goals; time pressures; and potentially severe consequences of poor decisions. Some earlier research highlighted how mismatches with decisions resulted strongly from insufficient decision maker experience, insufficient information, or incomplete or inadequate mental simulation.

Effective decision-making in crisis events is challenging due to time pressure, uncertainty, and dynamic decisional environments. A systematic literature review of 32 empirical research papers examined how trained professionals make naturalistic decisions under pressure in settings such as healthcare, military, fire and rescue, oil installation, and aviation domains. The main themes identified are: (1) decision-making strategy (2) time pressure (3) stress (4) uncertainty, and (5) errors. Recognition-primed decision-making (RPD) strategies were reported in all studies that analyzed this aspect. Analytical strategies were also prominent, appearing more frequently in contexts with less time pressure and explicit training to generate multiple explanations. Practitioner experience, time pressure, stress, and uncertainty were major influencing factors. Professionals must adapt to the time available, types of uncertainty, and individual skills when making decisions in high-risk situations. Improved understanding of these decisional factors can inform evidence-based enhancements to training, technology, and process design (Reale *et al.*, 2023).

In a typical case of non-compliance of PPE to the extent of 455 unsafe behaviours, though all were corrected on the spot, it was found that this non-compliance was due to lack of enforcement at the sites by project head, site engineers, contractors and so on. There was a sufficient disconnect with the risks involved in non-use of PPE or the perception that there is not enough potential for incidents. This case was discussed between the corporate business head, site heads, HSE professionals, and site engineers. It was conveyed that this is a collective failure and organisational cognitive error, not able to strike a balanced decision between the enforcement and the behavioural reinforcements at sites. All concerned took a decision to resolve this issue through mass-communications with the workers, and through corporate communications down to the site heads for their involvement to zero down this issue. Site heads were directly made responsible to mobilise actions to fix potential risks.

REFERENCES

Hutchinson, Ben (2022, Aug 31). Decision Errors and Accidents - Applying Naturalistic Decision Making to Accident Investigations.https://www.linkedin.com/pulse/decision-errors-accidents- applying-naturalistic-ben-hutchinson?trk=pulse-article_more-articles_related-content-card

Krasuski Adam, Mateusz Zimny, Simo Hostikka, Radosław Makowski (2022). Risk-aware decision making in the safety investments - Application of stochastic simulations and judgment value method. Fire Safety Journal, Volume 127,103491, ISSN 0379-7112. https://doi.org/10.1016/ j.firesaf.2021.103491.

Nadeem Muhammad Aamir, Surienty Lilis, Haque Md. Mahmudul (2022). Impact of organization decision making styles and safety accountability on occupational health and safety implementation: The moderating role of mimetic motives. Frontiers in Public Health,10. URL=https://www.frontiersin.org/articles/10.3389/fpubh.2022.1004767. DOI=10.3389/fpubh. 2022.1004767

Reale, Carrie *et al.,* (2023).Decision-Making During High-Risk Events: A Systematic Literature Review. Journal of Cognitive Engineering and Decision Making, 2023/02/18https://doi.org/10.1177/15553434221147415

Tata Steel (2021, March 15). Risk Profiling Turns Deep Shop Floor Experience into Enthusiastic Risk-Based Decision Making. https://www.consultdss.com/content-hub/risk-profiling-risk- based-decision-making/

12

Digitalising Positive Safety Culture

Organizations are now focused on creating a cohesive and agile workforce safety programme by implementing integrated, cloud-based EHS platforms. In other words, the digitization of safety has made it easier for companies to meet and exceed standards and requirements, and it has done so in a way that is itself safer for your employees and partners. Consider, for instance, that drones today can conduct inspections in difficult and dangerous conditions, allowing experts to view structures and sites remotely (Shuman, 2017).

Digitalising safety processes and checklists plays an essential role in driving your company's safety culture. Safety education underpins every safe workplace. Digitalising safety training provides organisations with a highly effective and consistent way to increase awareness, impart knowledge, and share best practice outcomes and successes (Branthonne, 2021).

The mechanisms for shaping the company safety culture through digital transformation, is now a key challenge for the entire global economy. From this cognitive perspective, it is important to define the place and role of digital transformation in shaping the safety culture.

Many organisations have developed mobile applications, QR codes for reporting safety observations. The use of artificial intelligence (AI), machine learning for workplace design are common but the safety effects of these interactions are not researched yet. For example, Uber ride is decided by the AI, but which driver would receive which customer is unknown, and is it going to be safe interaction between the both, is not covered in research so far.

Gopal Kumar, chief inspector of factories, Government of Jharkhand, on Thursday said that safety is multidimensional and cannot be defined. Since the formation of Factories and Mines Act, lots of work has been done in the field of safety and yet many more things need to be done. Around 7% of the world's population are working as engineers or as workers on sites which need to be alert and cautious during their work at shop floors. Addressing safety talks, he said that over 1000 severe incidents got registered last year and led to avoidable human deaths. He further stated that digitisation is the need of the hour for safety as it bridges the gap between man, process uncertainty and safety officers. Through the help of digitalisation, we can get insights of uncertainty and can get enough time to handle and avoid it. In coming times, digitisation would not be an option, it will be obligatory and part of our life. Probal Ghosh, vice president, shared services, Tata Steel Limited opined that synchronization of human, machinery and the workplace environment play a crucial role in the sustenance of any organization. Machinery accidents do happen in spite of adopting high tech processes because of behavioural issues. Hence, the attitude towards safety for both the employees and the top management is of utmost importance. Although risk cannot be completely eliminated, it can be reduced to an acceptable level through a systematic, process driven approach. Hence, we need to ensure that a robust safety management system is properly implemented in any organisation to provide safe working conditions for all its employees.

Ravi Ranjan, Director, ESL Steel Ltd said that behavioural safety is extremely important. Behaviour based safety programmes, when implemented correctly, can provide positive rewards to change unsafe behaviour, reduce job-related injuries, minimize lost production hours, and improve workplace morale. These are essential ingredients for creating a strong safety culture in any organisation. For making the workplace safer by eliminating hazards and preventing injuries, it requires a partnership between the company and its employees. For a company, its safety culture has the greatest impact on this partnership. Neeraj Kumar Sinha, Chief - Safety, Tata Steel Limited affirmed that commitment to safety is a value that shapes all decision-making at every level. A commitment to safety is constant effort towards transformation and is always about the next leg of the safety excellence journey. He further said that in our fight against the Covid pandemic, we have also seen how digital and technology has been the key enabler in managing the risks posed by the Coronavirus. Going forward, interventions such as artificial intelligence, data analytics, robotics, drones, etc., will become key enablers for controlling our workplace risks (*The Pioneer*, 2022).

BBS is the only solution available to control this behavioural shift and align it with safety regulations. BBS aims to positively reinforce behaviour by focusing on unravelling the reasons behind why and for what reasons we behave in a certain way and on creating a strategy to improve our behaviour. A BBS system encourages everyone within an organization to observe, report and comply with behavioural changes based on a thorough analysis of root cause, safety reports, and audits. A digitized BBS system will usher new levels of collaboration and analytics, ensuring a workplace that is constantly on the vigil to tackle safety issues and to find behavioural patterns that act as a deterrent for even future mishaps. With a digitized BBS application, industry can now report at-risk behaviour remotely using any device like mobile phones, tablets. In addition to universal reporting, a BBS application is the quickest approach to alert and streamline reporting to the delegated safety officers providing them with even multimedia observations like photos or videos. With a BBS software, employees ensure that you do not take a chance on safety by continuously monitoring behavioural trends and insights on observational targets to ensure they fall in line with company's safety principles. A BBS application with its organic statistical reports and deep analytical insights enables employees to manage risk and reduce at-risk behaviour by evaluating data observations of individuals or groups. BBS application comes with an easy-to-navigate user interface, simplifying the user experience of reporting and collaborating, making sure that the whole process is flexible. A digitized BBS system that is more relevant and easy to adopt, can create a more lasting impact on users and management to make safety more than just a mere choice, but a passion. A behaviour-based safety application garners the trust of individuals with its ability to perform when needed most. Through a culminated database intertwined with intelligent technology, individuals are automatically cautioned ahead of time through notifications and alerts (Nair, 2020).

REFERENCES

Branthonne, Denis (2021, May 11). 5 Ways Technology Is Improving Safety On Construction Sites. Https://Www.Novade.Net/5-Ways-Tech-Can-Improve-Safety-Construction/

Nair, Ramesh (2020, January 2). 5 Compelling Reasons To Digitize Behaviour Based Safety. Https://Www.Safetymint.Com/Blog/Digitize-Behaviour-Based-Safety/

Shuman, Natalia (2017, Dec 15). Digitizing Safety: A Closer Look At How Far Your Company Can Go. Https://Www.Linkedin.Com/Pulse/Digitizing-Safety-Closer-Look-How-Far-Your-Company- Can-Natalia-Shuman

The Pioneer (2022, November 11). C I I Safety Talks: Focus On Inculcating Safety Culture. Https://Www.Dailypioneer.Com/2022/State-Editions/Cii-Safety-Talks--Focus-On-Inculcating- Safety-Culture.Html

13

Success and Challenges of Positive Safety Culture

Good health and safety practices can have huge implications for business success. It can help achieve efficiency savings, boost profitability and secure contracts with larger companies. Importantly, by caring for staff, companies can also retain skilled and valuable workers. Creating a positive health and safety culture is a big challenge for businesses in India. A key step in creating a positive health and safety culture can be to make people aware of risks and how they can be managed (NEBOSH, 2017).

A successful positive safety culture connects everyone in the company around a common goal to measurably reduce near-misses and incidents. A positive safety culture is a strong differentiator in a competitive labour market to attract employees of all ages and skill sets. Commitment and communication are key aspects to a successful and positive safety culture in the workplace. A positive safety culture uses open communication to operate optimally in a singular direction that is clear to all throughout the company.

It is widely known that occupational health and safety is essential and obviously serves to secure workspaces to reduce accidents. However, several indirect benefits of a good OHS culture do exist and are not frequently discussed. Among these advantages, we find some that are directly related to the commercial success of a company. Indeed, a good OHS culture is often a sign of business success (Rouleau, 2021).

A serious gap in safety culture performance occurs when a passionate leader retires or leaves the company and nobody takes responsibility, as because it is not ensured that safety culture is an integral part of the management process. The degree to which an organization has already instilled a strong positive safety culture, is likely to influence organizational and individual perspectives on whether a specific good practice is viewed as a goal for the future, an already existing good practice norm of the organization (IAEA, 2023). For example, Thermax used 2 good practices: 'one day safety engineer' and 'sharing an incident before starting any meeting', which became an existing practice across its all businesses, a norm as well as future goal for sustaining the company's synergetic safety culture. A positive health and safety culture, embraced from the top to bottom, acts as a key enabler of organisational success. Ensuring occupational health and safety and minimising environmental impact are the foremost priorities of SEIL. We recognise that excellence in health, safety and environment is an ongoing journey and remain committed to implementing best practices, complying with internal Sembcorp HSE standards, as well as national and international standards. All our achievements and milestones in the last five years reflect our robust HSE management system and the true spirit in which it is implemented by all our staff. Management initiatives are massively improving staff commitment and participation in sustaining a positive health & safety culture (SEIL, 2023).

Success and challenges of positive safety culture depend upon factors such as:

1. Integration of positive safety culture with performance
2. Implementation of positive safety culture down the levels
3. Review of positive safety culture by topmost level
4. Reinforcement of positive safety culture by top management
5. Rewards and recognition of positive safety culture by site leadership

According to SEIL, the Challenges for Improving Safety Culture are:

- Every organisation is a business entity. It wants safety and productivity but there cannot be trade-off.
- According to Mr. Edgar Shien, Professor Emeritus, MIT Sloan says every employee comes to work with a combination cultures. Social culture that stops him from reporting on unsafe acts of his peers and has occupational culture based on hierarchy whether he is part of management, line management or associate. These social culture and occupational culture interact with safety culture.
- How management reacts to bad news matters. If management gets into "blame mode" then "learning" takes a hit.
- Typical Indian Psyche: It will not happen to me; I am doing this for a long time; I am very experienced. India ranks very low when it comes to safety institution & resources, safety frameworks and safety outcomes.
- Frontline is closest to hazard but has very little control over safety barriers.
- Proven research on short term memory says that human can remember 7 ± 2 things at a time and hence administrative controls are not as effective as we would like to imagine.
- People who work, assume they are in control, but it is the observer who always sees more hazards.
- Humans spend as much as 47% of their wakeup time thinking about something other than what they are doing.
- In 2000, an average human's attention span was 12 seconds. By 2015, it fell to 8.25 seconds. This impacts their ability to focus.

- India is 2nd most sleep deprived nation in world after Japan. Average Indian sleeps only 7.1 hours.
- Most Indian associates work in excess of 54 hours. So, fatigue plays a role.
- Human factors and human error are still not part of risk assessment.
- Every department including supporting departments like finance, HR and admin must contribute to safety.
- Lastly, companies need to fight complacency.

SEIL Safety Culture is committed to improve its Maturity

- Management's commitment being demonstrated by weekly monitoring, participation in discussions post-learning events, skip level safety townhalls and safety review meetings. Clear communication of what is acceptable and what will attract consequence management.
- Frontline safety is in prominence and since Jan 2021, monthly safety themes are focused on frontline safety which is being driven by management committee members.
- We engage with all stakeholders to develop co-operation and commitment to continually improve workplace safety by using concepts like psychological safety; human and organisational performance.
- We are trying to develop consistency and fight complacency. We make a conscious effort to continually improve.

SEIL Solutions for Improving Safety Culture

- Keep the BBS dynamic as per safety maturity level of organisation to address behaviours that need immediate attention.
- Continually make action plan to address top three hotspots of BBS.
- Divide hotspots into technical, general hotspots and assign actions to specific departments.

- Continual improvement to safety management system as soon as gap is noticed on ground.
- Have enough communication channels so that actionable points come to safety in real time.
- Nurture and mentor safety conscious employees and associates.
- Use all available resources to enhance field presence.
- Work on initiatives to plug the gaps.
- Ensure required competency, knowledge and awareness.
- Improve safety communications.
- Capture all learnings and share with all stakeholders.

Challenges to a positive safety culture include complexity, conflicts and behavioural problems. Solving specific health and safety issues can be complex in the workplace, as it involves the coordination of many people who carry out several different activities at the same time and requires in-depth knowledge and experience of the possible risks and consequences. Conflicts of interest between the objectives of the operation to obtain profits and, at the same time, guarantee the health and safety of people by respecting different types of standards / laws, as well as the law of protection of the environment. Sometimes people do not behave ideally and to maintain the level of health and safety, the worker must perform his work ideally. Sometimes they deliberately do something wrong and, therefore, health and safety standards are affected by the behaviour of workers (Safe World, 2023).

REFERENCES

IAEA (1997). Examples of Safety Culture Practices. International Atomic Energy Agency, Vienna, Safety Reports Series No. 1. https://www-pub.iaea.org/MTCD/publications/PDF/ STIPUB1039-70388427.pdf ISBN 92-0-104297-3. ISSN 1020-6450

NEBOSH (2017, November 17). Research shows culture can be a barrier to health and safety success in India. https://www.nebosh.org.uk/our-news-and-events/our-news/research-shows- culture-can-be-a-barrier-to-health-and-safety/

Rouleau, Francis (2021, Jan 5). The Benefits of a Positive Safety Culture. https://www.interventionprevention.com/en/the-benefits-of-a-positive-safety-culture/

Safe World (2023, February 04). Barriers to Positive Safety Culture. https://www.safeworldhse.com/2020/02/barriers-to-positive-safety-culture.html

SEIL (2023). Safety at the Core. https://www.sembcorpenergyindia.com/AnnualReport2020/safety-at-the-core.php

14

Total Safety Culture Interventions

In simple words, safety culture is to getting employees to work as a team, as a workplace incident or safety or zero-harm perspective calls for a unified response of an organisation. A safety professional's ultimate goal is to achieve a total safety culture (TSC) in an organisation.

The EHS professionals who are aware have now begun to unravel and demand robust safety measures. When companies facing a reactive safety culture, they suffer from all issues pertaining to unsafe behaviour, psychological safety, human factors, human error, cultural safety and so on. As soon as, they implement positive safety culture as a long-term planned intervention, and they go over towards next level of cultural maturity from reactive and dependent to independent and interdependent safety culture, organizations begin to manage all these issues of unsafe behaviour, psychological safety, human factors, human error, cultural safety. Nevertheless, it is a sheer hard work and continuous journey to capture risks and control them on the spot before walking over the same. The EHS fraternity keeps updating on the new areas of implementation so that they are in touch with international safety standards. Implementation can only give better control over challenges whatsoever. All depends upon how fast the topmost management is ready to engage in the pressing safety issues to resolve, and the corporate HSE professionals deeply understood to act upon the organizational scenario and antecedents changes required.

A safety professional's ultimate goal is to achieve a total safety culture (TSC) within his/her organization. In a TSC, everyone feels responsible for safety and pursues it on a daily basis; employees go beyond "the call of duty" to identify unsafe conditions and behaviours, and intervene to correct them. In a TSC, safe work practices are supported via rewarding feedback from peers and managers; people "actively care" on a continuous basis for safety. In a TSC, safety is not a priority that can be shifted depending on situational demands; rather, safety is a value linked with all other situational priorities (ProQuest, 2023).

During the implementation follow-ups of behavioural safety, we need to also review the critical influences of organizational culture, i.e., psychological safety aspects, human factors, human errors, cultural safety in an overall context of a dynamic organization.

Total Safety Culture (TSC) Interventions

1. Robust safety systems: reinforcing antecedents for managing all safety issues such as barriers, resources, safety controls.
2. Safety culture: long-term behavioural interventions with fast-tracking action plan.
3. Psychological safety: do people feel psychologically safe?
4. Human factors of safety: do people feel very strained with occupational stresses, workload, decision latitude issues?

5. Human error in safety: human cognition, decision making, fear, pressure. How companies handle group conflicts and differences that delay safety culture decisions.
6. Cultural safety and competency: do people feel being understood with their cultural background and beliefs, and how companies respond to these factors effectively?
7. Digitalising safety measures, AI, machine learning, more innovations.
8. Integrating and reviews by the topmost leaders on all the above interventions.

Many organisations continue to face incidents as they implement only a part of the total/ideal/optimal safety culture interventions. It is important to understand how companies respond to the challenges associated with each of these safety culture interventions over a long period of time and integrate or sustain them in their respective organisational dynamics and framework. Daily reinforcement of safe behaviour by all employees make it easier for enforcement of safety rules and regulations.

In total safety culture, all personnel do not merely care about workplace safety, they actively care about the health, safety, and wellbeing of their fellow employees, as well as the broader community. They do not wait for an injury to occur before taking action, but instead they proactively search for hazards, at-risk behaviours, and system factors that increase the probability of an injury. Any observed at-risk behaviour is viewed as a symptom of a potential systemic issue lying deeper within the organization. They continuously make or suggest improvements to keep people safe and strengthen defenses before anyone gets hurt. In a TSC, employees at all levels of the organizational hierarchy have become brother/sister of human welfare, wellbeing, and life satisfaction. Behavioural safety focuses on direct observations of behaviour to identify ways to cultivate a safe workplace, whereas safety culture surveys use focus groups to ascertain system factors to address (EHS Daily Advisor, 2018). All employees and workmen are trained to look for safety issues and communicate freely for immediate rectifications without delays.

Positive safety psychology is the key to all total zero harm perspectives and implementation of TSC in the workplaces or elsewhere. The EHS departments remain understaffed all over the world. While implementing positive safety culture methodology, every one at workplace is actively careful to support on safety and wellbeing issues of their colleagues.

Strategies found to enhance the safety culture include exchange of experiences and learnings, integration of staff's perceptions, external facilitation, staff training, and a structured, multi-step procedure of the intervention process. Some studies were unable to show statistically significant enhancement in safety culture from the interventions implemented. Factors facilitating the implementation of interventions include good connections and trust between staff and managers, and the manager's active support of the project goals, as well as targeting achievable ideas considering time and resources. Time pressure, heavy workloads and high staff turnover may inhibit the process. Overall, there was considerable heterogeneity in interventions aiming to enhance safety culture. Despite these aspects, promising approaches are training staffs knowledge and competencies regarding open communication and teamwork as part of a multifaceted programme. Future research would benefit from participative, carefully developed, comprehensively evaluated interventions for enhancing safety culture. Key learning points are the change management, intervention implementation, long-term care, and safety culture systematic reviews. Recognising safety risks and promoting safe care is essential and should be an integral part of the overall preventive endeavours. The safety culture describes efforts regarding the acknowledgement and reduction of safety risks. Enhanced safety culture in organisations can be associated with a lower incidence of missed observations and adverse events (Garay *et al.*, 2023).

REFERENCES

EHS Daily Advisor (2018, Aug 6). Safety Culture 2018: The Human Dynamics of Cultivating a Total Safety Culture—A Q&A with E. Scott Geller and Steve Roberts. https:// ehsdailyadvisor.blr.com/2018/08/safety-culture-2018-human-dynamics-cultivating-total- safety-culture-qa-e-scott-geller-steve-roberts/

Garay Sandra, Mathias Haeger, Laura Kühnlein, Daniela Sulmann, Ralf Suhr, (2023). Interventions to enhance safety culture for nursing professionals in long-term care: A systematic review. International Journal of Nursing Studies Advances, Volume 5, 100119, ISSN 2666-142X. https://doi.org/10.1016/j.ijnsa.2023.100119.

ProQuest (2023). Ten principles for achieving a total safety culture. https://www.proquest.com/docview/200347593

15

Linking Safety Behaviour to Key Performance Indicators (KPI)

Behaviour is the seed of safety culture, hence it is reasonable to be linked to KPIs. Like with one seed, we can grow thousands of fruits and more seeds, similarly with behavioural KPI of an individual employee and actions, we save thousands of lives from incidents, and prevent injuries innumerable. Hence, behavioural KPI on occupational health and safety (OHS) needs more emphasis by managers and to be implemented by the workers at all sites.

The businesses and industries have taken human safety on path of unsafe events. So the losses had to be borne by way of fatalities, injuries, diseases, so on. Safety is inherent in the nature and blood of every human being. Companies have to make it a part of workers performance and importantly, the managers team monitors and reinforces it daily. Employees KPIs turn into organisational performance which depends upon the organisational future goals.

KPIs provide an eyeful and mindful direction to the workers as to what they should look for each day at site in order to ensure the health and safety of self and employees around. For implementation of safety key performance indicators, the organizational factors and control mechanisms are potential to increase the level of safety (Lalis and Vittek, 2014).

Even organisations with low lost time injury (LTI) can experience catastrophic injuries, so KPIs should be set that delve further into a workplace's safety maturity. Looking beyond accident rates to ensure the workforce is not just reacting to hazards, rather than simply anticipating them, is an important cultural factor to embed into a company's ethos. Regularly reviewing KPIs will help ensure continual improvement of workplace health and safety. Consider gaps in coverage to ensure nothing is being missed and assess whether your KPIs are balanced and give the correct emphasis to the most pertinent issues (Fletcher, 2019).

First and foremost are safety KPIs. Managing safety KPIs should be the top priority for any project manager. Safety key performance indicators are measurements of the different parts and processes of your safety programmes. The key performance indicators at the workplace impact positively or negatively the quality of life. The purpose is to explore the maturity in all health and safety care services to improve outcomes (Nafouri, 2020).

KPIs when measuring behavioural safety: Use participation rates with caution means getting people on board with your behavioural safety measures is one of the key challenges when it comes to implementing a new policy. Analyse the number of potential or serious injuries and fatalities, so a low percentage in this KPI is usually a good indicator of behavioural safety change if the figure has gone down.

Corrective action rate: This is good for measuring to what extent behavioural safety measures have influenced the degree to which work has to be corrected to be deemed safe. If there is a fall in the number of corrective actions, this is an indication that behavioural safety measures have worked to some extent.

Use metrics with caution: Whilst the different metrics listed have been tested and can be useful when evaluating the performance of behavioural safety measures, as with many data points they can be misleading and only tell part of the story. This is why it is important to consider any different aspects of performance, be it through worker feedback and lived experiences as part of a holistic measurement of behavioural safety (HSE Network, 2020).

For corporate health and safety culture management performance, we look into the KPIs as how well they are defined for each individual employee as a quantifiable measure, to review and track whether their key business objectives are on track, behind, ahead, or have been achieved. These individual or personal, departmental, and contractors' KPIs are set and appraised monthly/quarterly so that the feedback can be provided by the managers to employees to enhance their OHS performance with adequate mentoring. OHS KPIs must be kept short and simple, realistic, observable, measurable, achievable and time-bound (Fouche, 2021).

Safety culture is a culture of care. Workplace culture priorities for 2023 include doubling down on care for workers. So how would companies link individuals' actively caring pattern to performance indicators across the month? Whether employees performed behaviours of caring and supporting colleagues through their daily safety actions such as observations and corrections of at-risk behaviours, hazards, barriers using a brother or sister approach? For improving business outcomes, make key performance indicators (KPIs) well informed for quantitative decisions, and adopting a strategic approach to benchmarking. Corporate leaders are aware of the importance of monitoring and calculating employee KPIs, and those looking to accelerate growth will be keen to broaden their focus on metrics that measure project and company-wide performance in safer perspectives (Davidson, 2023). Convert organization's strategic objectives into your employees KPIs and boost gross revenue.

Key risk indicators (KRIs) or safety performance indicators (SPIs) are used by organisations to determine how much risk they are exposed to. Before deciding KPIs, it is essential to know the KRIs, though both KPI and SPI are deeply correlated. A key risk indicator is a metric for measuring the likelihood that the combined probability of an event and its consequences. Key risk indicators play an important role in enterprise risk management programmes. Benefits of KRIs include the advance notice of potential risks that could damage the organisation, insights into organisation's risk monitoring, controls and risk assessments. Key risk indicators are critical predictors of unfavourable events, hence each KRI should be linked to a KPI (Kirvan, 2023).

Behaviours are the root cause of almost all incidents, accidents as well as unsafe conditions. Hence the behavioural safety indicators (BSIs) for organisations are very important for accounting at-risk behaviours, hazards, barriers, resources as well as organisational antecedents. For evolving positive safety culture, organisations need to set behavioural tools, indicators and standards as described below.

1. Training and re-training of the manpower on behavioural safety implementation.
2. Setting daily goals for reduction of at-risk behaviours, hazards, barriers, resources.
3. Daily tool box talk (TBT) and reverse TBT.
4. Daily mass communications on at-risk behaviours, hazards, barriers, resources.
5. Daily observations rounds for spot-correction of at-risk behaviours.
6. Weekly review of BSI.
7. Time bound rectification of hazards, barriers, resources.
8. Display of BSI progress every month by departments.
9. Reporting BSI progress to top management.
10. Quarterly review of BSI progress by the Board of Directors.

REFERENCES

Davidson, Neil (2023, Feb 02). Why KPIs will be more important than ever this year. https://www.newcivilengineer.com/latest/why-kpis-will-be-more-important-than-ever-this- year-02-02-2023/

Fletcher, Jamie (2019, Oct 28). How To Set KPIS For Health And Safety. Https:// Www.Linkedin.Com/Pulse/How-Set-Kpis-Health-Safety-Jamie-Fletcher-Contego-Safety- Solutions-

Fouche Christel (2021, Oct 13). Occupational Health and Safety KPIs. https:// www.linkedin.com/pulse/occupational-health-safety-kpis-christel-fouche?trk=pulse- article_more-articles_related-content-card

HSE Network (2020, August 26). Some of the 'key performance indicators' when measuring behavioural safety. https://www.hse-network.com/some-of-the-key-performance-indicators-when-measuring-behavioural-safety/

Kirvan, Paul (2023). key risk indicator (KRI). https://www.techtarget.com/searchcio/definition/key-risk-indicator-KRI

Lalis, Andrej & Vittek, Peter (2014). Safety KPIs - Monitoring of safety performance. MAD - Magazine of Aviation Development. 2. 9. 10.14311/MAD.2014.11.02.

Nafouri, Nashat (2020, Jan 06). Moving from KPI TO HDI. https://insights.omnia-health.com/hospital-management/moving-kpi-hdi

16

Human Factors and Human Error in Safety Culture

Error is an unintentional deviation from safe practice. Multiple errors combine to result in a major catastrophe. Near-miss is an error that has the potential to cause an adverse event but fails to do so because of chance or because it is intercepted. Keeping track of near-misses gives insight into loopholes in the system and helps in designing multiple checkpoints to prevent the catastrophe. Errors are unintentional. If the deviation from safe practice is intentional, it is termed violation. Human errors or cognitive errors form a significant portion of preventable mishaps in industry. Even the most competent professionals are not immune to it. Errors can often have grave consequences, and hence, the experts need to be aware of the impact of human errors and how to minimise them. Errors are broadly classified into two kinds: latent and active errors. While active errors need to be addressed at the individual level, latent errors indicate organisational inadequacies (Vattipalli *et al.*, 2021).

Human failure is normal and predictable. It can be identified and managed. Industry should tackle error reduction in a structured and proactive way. A human error is an action or decision which was not intended. A violation is a deliberate deviation from a rule or procedure. Some errors are slips or lapses, often actions that were not as planned or unintended actions. They occur during a familiar task and include slips (pressing the wrong button or reading the wrong gauge) and lapses (forgetting to carry out a step in a procedure). These can be eliminated by behavioural observations training for employees to actively care for each other. Other errors are mistakes or errors of judgement or decision-making where the intended actions are wrong, i.e., where we do the wrong thing believing it to be right. These tend to occur in situations where the person does not know the correct way of carrying out a task either because it is new and unexpected, or because they have not been properly trained (or both). Training based on good procedures is the key to avoiding mistakes. Violations (non-compliances, shortcuts) are intentional where the person deliberately does not carry out the procedure correctly. Mistakes resulting from poor training (people have not been properly trained in the safe working procedure) are often mistaken for violations. Organisational factors such as peer pressure, unworkable rules and incomplete understanding, interpersonal conflicts can give rise to violations. Everyone can make errors no matter how well trained and motivated they are. However in the workplace, the consequences of such human failure can be severe. Analysis of accidents and incidents shows that human failure contributes to almost all accidents and exposures to substances hazardous to health. Many major accidents such as Bhopal, Chernobyl were initiated by human failure. In order to avoid accidents and ill-health, companies need to manage human failure or errors as robustly as the technical and engineering measures they use for that purpose (Health and Safety Executive, 2023).

In recent years, studies on the causes of accidents in various industries and fields have consistently shown that human errors or human factors play a decisive role in accidental property losses and casualties. Therefore, the key to strengthening accident prevention is to reduce human errors at the source, and some studies have shown that safety culture has a positive impact on the safety behaviour performance of enterprise employees (Pei *et al.*, 2023).

Human error is an individual response to an unsafe or at-risk behaviour in the context of an organisation whichever way you define it, let it be behaviour, barrier or resource, etc. For example, when Mr Bindra a company director stops at an unsafe condition, he wants to respond to it immediately and correct it. But the site head says that does not matter, we go ahead, my engineer would close the issue. But the director maintains that he would not walk on until it is corrected. Look at the response to human error which is at the cognitive level in terms of risk perception and immediate rectification. The cognition differential level of the two positions has to merge and culminate at a higher level of safety response and decision making for sending a positive message down the level who all are witnessing the safety scene that the correction is immediate whatever is the risk, howsoever you define it, no one can delay closing the risk there and then.

Similarly, the cognition level of safety culture can be exemplified when an operator sees a person falling into a container at a height, he responds immediately, brings him back on the ground, calls the doctor, and revives the person. When it comes to rewarding, the doctor is rewarded, not the operator. The cognitive error in safety culture sets in. The negative thinking of this operator who saved a contract workman, is that in future he would not endeavour saving a person, let the doctor do it. A positive organisational response need to be that the reward in this situation has to be given to both the operator and the doctor, not to one person alone, in order to avoid such a human error setting in. Another example, when a security guy overcomes the fire in a flat in the building saving the entire assets. The reward is so meagre that it does not motivate him to remain proactive. In another situation, when a general manager emphasises more on completing targets to his DGM colleagues than reinforcing safety. It sets a cognitive error. It matters significantly as to how the higher bosses tackle the situation to balance the targets and safety respectfully. Thereafter, the executive director sees to it that it is clarified between them in order to avoid any such error. At the same level, when a HSE guy comes up with an issue of conflict with the customer or business client at a site. The business head immediately comes forward to offer him support, saying that he should fix his meeting with the customer, and he would intervene respectfully to resolve it immediately.

Human factors in safety culture, on the other hand, refers to the occupational stress and mental health issues that requires an organisational response to manage such scenarios positively.

Human factors (positive or negative) are the organisational factors or situations that impact the people's actions and mindset. Supportive factors would reinforce safety culture, whereas the negative/reactive factors impede the safety behaviours of the workers. Managers and supervisors need to be trained to positively deal with stress and mental health issues of the employees for augmenting safety culture. Similarly, the situational factors like time pressure, fear, lack of resources create a mindset that nobody takes safety decisions, and safety culture takes a back seat, and incidents creep in taking toll on people and property. How organisations and the leadership respond in such situations, matters most in re-building positive vibes for safety culture.

REFERENCES

Health and Safety Executive (2023). Human factors: Managing human failures. https://www.hse.gov.uk/humanfactors/topics/humanfail.htm

Pei, J.; Liu, L.; Chi, Y.; Yu, C. Research on the Maturity Evaluation Model of Enterprise Safety Culture. *Int. J. Environ. Res. Public Health* **2023**, *20*,2664. https://doi.org/10.3390/ ijerph20032664

Vattipalli Sameera, Bindra A, Rath GP. (2021). Human errors and their prevention in healthcare. J Anaesthesiol Clin Pharmacol. 2021 Jul-Sep;37(3):328-335. doi: 10.4103/ joacp.JOACP_364_19. Epub 2021 Oct 12. PMID: 34759539; PMCID: PMC8562433.

17

Cultural Safety and Diversity

Cultural safety refers to ensuring safe environments for cultural modes of life that differ from the dominant normative conventions of a society. The 'cultural' refers to socioeconomic status, age, gender, sexual orientation, ethnic origin, migrant/refugee status, religious beliefs, disability, LGBTQIA+, professional cultures, and so on. Diversity is an objective, with cultural safety about indigenous peoples worldwide, multicultural communities, immigrant communities, and culturally and linguistic diverse communities, and in all countries (MDPI, 2023).

Cultural safety is more than the absence of racism, it is the "positive recognition and celebration of cultures… that empowers people and enables them to contribute and feel safe to be themselves" (NSW, 2023).

Cultural safety and diversity (CSD) is addressed to see that the workers, especially at the lowest level, are being listened to and understood with due respect to their cultural background, beliefs and language, for ensuring development of positive safety culture. In India, some organisations celebrate the local cultural and religious festivals (such as Raksha Bandhan, Ganesha Puja, Diwali, Christmas and so on) inside the plant settings to maintain a psychological and social connect for the purpose of workers' safety and wellbeing. CSD recognises cultural differences and is sensitive to the cultural traditions, protocols and customs. Health and safety systems need to be engaged in working towards cultural safety. To do this, they must be prepared to critique the taken for granted power structures and be prepared to challenge their own culture and cultural systems rather than prioritise becoming competent in the cultures of others. The objective of cultural safety activities also needs to be clearly linked to achieving health and safety equity. Organisations and authorities need to be held accountable for providing culturally safe care. Internationally, indigenous and minority ethnic groups experience inequities in their access to and receipt of high quality health and safety care. The cultural competency and cultural safety are now key areas of concern and issues around how to define these terms have become paramount, in order to better inform both local and international contexts (Curtis *et al.*, 2019).

The concept of 'Culturally Safe' is critical in enhancing personal empowerment to help provide a safe environment which includes cultural safety, which means that there is no assault on a person's identity. The people most able or equipped to provide a culturally safe atmosphere are people from the same culture. To genuinely address the challenges. Defining or framing a debate on cultural safety is essential. Committing to cultural safety in your workplace will help you to understand yourself, your values and attitudes that may affect others (Robyn, 1999). It would help understand to what an extent, people value or do not value safety in their personal life, so as to decide an action plan with them to develop safety culture. It helps creation and maintenance of culturally safe workplaces especially for contract workmen. Contract workers are a vulnerable population when it comes to serious injuries and fatalities on the job. With contractors often performing higher-risk jobs with little to no supervision, it is a best practice for employers to have a formal contractor management programme (NSC, 2023).

Cultural safety is also about understanding and addressing health and social inequities that exist between peoples of different cultures or economic backgrounds or minority groups or temporary workers. A culturally safe workplace provides all workers with a workplace that has respectful communication, two-way dialogue, an environment that values all contributions, recognition and avoidance of stereotypical barriers, and shared knowledge. Many employers and managers believe their workplace is culturally safe, but, in fact, it misses the mark. They don't see the subtle indicators that point to the organisation being culturally insensitive. It often takes an expert in the field to come into an organisation to highlight areas that can be improved (Stephens, 2021).

How do we foster cultural safety in the workplace is a critical query? Cultural safety is more than being aware of other cultures and respecting their people. It is an environment where people of diverse cultural and ethnic backgrounds can feel respected and safe - spiritually, socially, emotionally, and physically - from discrimination and denial of their identity and needs. Developing cultural safety is a journey that takes time and commitment. In order to achieve cultural safety, we must progress through five steps of awareness. Cultural awareness is the start of the journey, where we recognise that differences and similarities exist between cultures. Cultural sensitivity grows when we start to see the influences of our own culture and acknowledge that we have biases. With cultural awareness and sensitivity comes a responsibility to act respectfully. Cultural competency is about building an understanding of other cultures and developing practical skills for interacting in respectful ways with people who are different from ourselves. Cultural competency does not require us to become experts in other cultures but we are responsible for reducing the number of assumptions we make about people based on our biases – whether intentional or not. Cultural humility is the most important step towards working in a culturally safe way. Moving through cultural awareness, cultural sensitivity, and cultural competency through cultural humility, as individuals, and as an organisation is one of the most effective ways to enable cultural safety (VPSO, 2021).

A culturally safe workplace has a defined set of values and principles, and demonstrates behaviours, attitudes, policies, and structures that enable all workers to work effectively cross-culturally. In a culturally safe workplace all workers feel comfortable, supported and respected. Cultural safety means everyone, regardless of culture, needs to be treated with respect, inclusion, and transparent management and health and safety policies (NSW, 2023).

There is a strong correlation between workplace diversity and inclusion (D&I) and improved business performance, propelling the implementation of D&I programmes. Organisations are increasingly implementing strategies encouraging D&I. Cultural safety requires ensuring that employees are secure and given the ability to flourish, regardless of race, religion, gender, physical or intellectual differences, or sexuality (BOB, 2023).

REFERENCES

BOB (2023). Cultural Safety For HR Leaders. https://www.hibob.com/guides/cultural-safety-guide/

Curtis E, Jones R, Tipene-Leach D, Walker C, Loring B, Paine SJ, Reid P. Why cultural safety rather than cultural competency is required to achieve health equity: a literature review and recommended definition. Int J Equity Health. 2019 Nov 14;18(1):174. doi: 10.1186/s12939-019-1082-3. PMID:31727076; PMCID: PMC6857221.

MDPI (2023). Cultural Safety – towards a Global Research Agenda. https://www.mdpi.com/topics/cultural_safety

NSC (2023). Keeping Contractors Safe. https://www.nsc.org/work-safety/services/research/contractor-safety

NSW (2023). What is cultural safety? https://www.safework.nsw.gov.au/safety-starts-here/our-aboriginal-programme/culturally-safe-workplaces/what-is-cultural-safety

NSW (2023). Cultural Safety and Wellbeing: Critical elements. https://evidenceportal.dcj.nsw.gov.au/evidence-portal-home/our-evidence-reviews/cultural-safety-and-wellbeing/critical-elements.html

Robyn, Williams (1999). Cultural safety - What does it mean for our work practice?. Australian and New Zealand Journal of Public Health. 23. 213 - 214. 10.1111/j.1467-842X.1999.tb01240.x.

Stephens, Anya (2021, December 21). Understanding Cultural Safety in the Workplace Mental Health. https://www.peoplesense.com.au/news/article/21122021-239/understanding-cultural-safety-in-the-workplace

VPSO (2021). How do we foster cultural safety in the workplace is a critical query? https://vpfo.ubc.ca/2021/04/how-do-we-foster-cultural-safety-in-the-workplace/

18

Integrating Total Safety Culture Interventions with Organisational Behaviour

Integrating and sustaining safety culture require a controlled focus on several levels of influence on worker safety and wellbeing, as the relationship between work and safety is never unidirectional. Total safety culture imbibes as policies, programmes, and practices that integrate protection from work-related safety and health hazards with promotion of injury and illness prevention efforts to advance worker's wellbeing. Integrated interventions of health and safety outcomes would include workplace safety, quality of life, physical and psychological wellbeing, cultural safety, human factors, human errors, health symptoms, and stress. Characteristics of effective integrated interventions include the intervention development, implementation, and outcomes (Bradley *et al.*, 2016).

Integration means learning to practise safety on daily basis and reviewing to sustain the outcomes.

After changing their focus to culture, the manufacturing company showed 14 years of continuous improvement, won numerous safety awards, and surpassed the performance of some of their benchmarking peers. That's the impact of culture as applied to safety (Steven, 2020). Everyone raises voice for safety, safety culture comes and risk disappears, is it so simple? Most companies delayed their HSE decisions till they suffered. Why so? Without inculcating safety as a core corporate value, industry cannot be considered safe.

Workplace fatality rate has reached at a frightening point, where 2.3 million causalties and 1.9 million severe injuries showing an increasing trend. In response to these figures, organisations are getting more concerned toward employees' safety and respective parameters (Hafeez *et al.*, 2022).

Safety culture is a social construct, gradually gets shaped over time by multilevel influences such as values, assumptions, norms and behaviours used to enact them. These influences framework synthesises information across fragmented conceptualisations to clearly depict the dynamic nature of safety culture and specific drivers of its development. Safety culture development may depend on employee learning from behavioural outcomes, conducive enabling factors, consistency over time, and the dynamic processes involved (Bisbey *et al.*, 2019). When employees learning of the safety culture is being practised on daily basis, it starts becoming an integral part of the work culture. Safety culture is a part of organisational culture. So integrating safety culture would mean to sustain it in the culture and nature of an organisation. Therefore, before defining a safety culture, it is essential to understand the cultural diversity of an organisation. Companies must develop a sustainable-oriented organizational culture (Jasiulewicz-Kaczmarek, 2022).

In companies with strong safety cultures, safety is embedded in daily management, and it is part of the fabric of daily activity. It infuses every interaction, every decision and every behaviour.

Unfortunately, in many organisations, leaders only attend to safety during safety meetings, audits and respond reactively, when there is an incident. Integrating safety culture needs to reflect in daily actions of all employees. Companies that embed safety as a core value, integrated into every aspect of work, are able to demonstrate not only their commitment to worker safety but a consistent improvement in results because safety is widely visible. Safety is everyone's responsibility, and every job, function and department plays a role, from top to bottom (Sears and Sullivan, 2023).

Integrating and sustaining total safety culture interventions would involve a self-evaluation by company leaders/employees on where are we now, and where to go, and how to go? This exercise would provide qualitative data, themes and directions about improving and sustaining the safety culture. Creating a safety culture among your workforce is among the easiest and most sustainable ways to minimise the occurrence of hazardous incidents in your organisation. By inculcating safety as a core value in workers by regular safety education, organisations can ensure that everyone actively adheres to safety regulations and practices (British Safety Council, India, 2020).

The areas of strength of integrating sustainable total safety culture include teamwork within and across units, organisational learning, managerial support, overall perception of safety, feedback and communication about error, non-punitive response to error, and openness. These aspects led to visible changes in the safety culture and consistent leadership commitment and support. Safety culture dimensions to integrate are the organisational factors, changes and barriers affecting the safety culture. Perhaps there is no leadership responsibility more profound than creating a sustainable, injury-free workplace (Titi, *et al.*, 2021).

Challenges in sustaining total Safety Culture can be overcome by consistent behavioural safety education, re-training, reinforcement by leaders, support, follow-ups, and multi-level reviews.

Geller stated (Safety Culture, 2023) that there are three factors that reflect a total safety culture: internal personal factors, external environmental factors, and behaviour factors. These factors need to be present at all times. Fundamental to BBS, the integrated approach is based upon Geller's seven principles. This integrated approach utilizes both individual and organizational behaviour which helps achieve the total safety culture. The following are the seven principles: The behaviour interventions should be observable. Determine external factors that can help understand and improve behaviours. Antecedents should be used to direct behaviours while consequences should be used to motivate behaviour. Highlight positive consequences to reinforce favourable behaviours. Make sure that the BBS programme is measurable and objective. Do not limit possibilities, create hypotheses and combine information gathered from the BBS programme. Create a BBS programme that considers employees' feelings and attitudes.

REFERENCES

Bisbey, Tiffany M. Kilcullen, Molly P. Thomas, Eric J. Ottosen, Madelene J. Tsao, K. Salas, Eduardo (2019). Safety Culture: An Integration of Existing Models and a Framework for Understanding Its Development. Human Factors. doi: 10.1177/0018720819868878

Bradley Cathy J., David C. Grossman, Rebecca A. Hubbard, *et al.* (2016). Integrated Interventions for Improving Total Worker Health: A Panel Report From the National Institutes of Health Pathways to Prevention Workshop: Total Worker Health—What's Work Got to Do With It?. Ann Intern Med.165:279-283. [Epub 31 May 2016]. doi:10.7326/ M16-0740

British Safety Council, India (2020, April 27). How to build a safety culture in the workplace. https://www.britsafe.in/publications-and-blogs/ blogs/read-all-blogs/how-to-build-a-safety- culture-in-the-workplace/

Jasiulewicz-Kaczmarek, M.; Antosz, K.; Wyczółkowski, R.; Sławin ska,M. **(2022).** IntegratedApproach for Safety Culture Factor Evaluation from a Sustainability Perspective. *Int. J. Environ. Res. Public Health, 19*, 11869. https://doi.org/10.3390/ ijerph191911869

Hafeez, H., Abdullah, M.I., Zaheer, M.A. and Ahsan, Q. (2022), "Organizational resilience process: integrated model of safety culture", Organization Management Journal , Vol. 19 No. 1, pp. 2-21. https:// doi.org/10.1108/OMJ-03-2020-0893

Safety Culture (2023, Jan 31). Behaviour Based Safety. https://safetyculture. com/topics/behaviour- based-safety/

Sears, Don and Sullivan, Julie (2023). To Integrate Safety Culture, Focus On Changing Behaviour. https://www.mscdirect.com/betterMRO/safety/ integrate-safety-culture-focus- changing-behaviour

Steven Simon (2020, Nov 10). Integrating Organisational Culture And Safety Performance. https://www.humansynergistics.com/blog/culture-university/details/culture-university/2020/11/10/integrating-organizational-culture-and-safety-performance

Titi Ma, Baksh Mm, Zubairi B, Et Al (2021). Staying Ahead Of The Curve: Navigating Changes And Maintaining Gains In Patient Safety Culture - A Mixed-Methods Studybmj Open 2021;11:E044116. Doi: 10.1136/Bmjopen-2020-044116

19

Fixing Accountability Levels to Mobilise Positive Safety Culture

Organisations document the risk, but don't take action. Documenting the risk is important but if you don't take action to mitigate it, it is riskier. Many serious incidents happened when organisations knew the risk as documented, but they did not take action to close the same. Hence, organisations and managers need to evaluate accountability for the persons responsible on this critical gap for mobilising positive and proactive safety culture.

Often leaders do not perform as they are not held responsible for change process and its results. They attend meetings but do not contribute meaningfully. They need to be challenged and stimulated mentally on regular basis for their active involvement on company goals. They need not be left as onlookers. The meeting's chairperson must realise that others' involvement need to be demanded for actions required.

People try often to fix others accountable, but not themselves, even for right things to be done. But the cultural change demands that everyone top to bottom is accountable for positive safety culture for their company, people, and doing business for which they are paid. If folks are to be held fairly accountable for their results, they have to have a clear idea of just what is expected of us in terms of our behaviour and what those results are supposed to be. Coach and train people to those objectives and expectations. The reality is that oftentimes performance objectives are in fact not clearly specified, and are not automatically understood, such that willing, well-intentioned workers may fail to do the right things, for no real fault of their own. Measure and evaluate performance on an ongoing basis. Give ongoing feedback. Appraise safety performance. Honor commitments (Kello, 2010).

A strong safety culture means nothing if your employees aren't motivated on a personal level. Make safety part of overall accountability. Seek employee input and feedback. Empower even the lowest in the hierarchy. Make safety part of evaluations. Ensure management knows the cost of an unsafe workplace. Get some analytics to show the company's managing director just how much money they can save by implementing a safe working culture (Safety Culture Team, 2018).

Employee buy-in is crucial to have a positive safety culture. Implementing a clear accountability process can aid a positive safety culture. By having responsible persons for health and safety procedures can help with accountability and promote the metrics of leading by example. An example of this would be the capabilities of dealing with a crisis and learning from them through strong safety culture. Organizations with strong safety cultures understand that emergencies and incidents could occur at any time and have robust systems in place to immediately deal with them. They have effective methods of communicating those incidents internally and have the methodologies and the know-how to investigate and understand their root causes. Most importantly, they lead by example by learning from these incidents and ensuring it never happens again. When developing or revising safety policies, make sure that you involve employees throughout the process. This not only ensures that their voices are heard, but it also helps them understand why certain measures have been put in place and how they can contribute to a culture of safety within the organisation (Tanya, 2020).

Evaluating for accountability: OSHA looks primarily for two programme elements when evaluating an employer for accountability: Policy and consequences. OSHA does not mandate or require specific recognition/disciplinary procedures: That's the responsibility of the employer. But, an effective accountability policy that is written and clearly communicated should be in place. Make sure your company has a written policy that addresses accountability including the three key components: specific performance expectations, who is accountable – both management and employee, appropriate consequences such as progressive discipline. If you believe there are weaknesses in your employer's accountability system, make sure to take notes on the behaviours and conditions you see in the workplace that may be pointing to accountability system policies, plans, processes, and procedures that are inadequate or missing (Ali, 2021).

Accountability, equality, encouragement, teamwork, and training are the 5 elements of safety culture (Hanson, 2022). All the five works in tandem for building best work culture, and accountability becomes the function of the interaction of the other four elements. A behavioural- based, data-informed safety culture boosts operational efficiency and improves worker accountability to a higher level. Creating and fostering accountability in the workplace is an important part of improving the safety culture of an organization.

Think of accountability for yourself first, followed by accountability of others. Accountability is a shared practice – the leader and the employee each have a part. A major pitfall with accountability is unclear expectations. Many times, we assume expectations are understood. Check your assumptions. Have explicit discussions on expectations to minimize misunderstandings. The benefits of accountability are building your capability to get things done yourself, enabling the accomplishments of others and positively changing the culture in your workgroup (Angelo, 2022).

It is important to ensure all employees are accountable for their actions if they fail to follow and comply with safety rules and instructions. A safety culture cannot be created or thrive without managers and workers being held accountable for unsafe or unhealthy actions. Individuals should be formally required to follow the safety rules and be held accountable if they fail to do so. By conducting regular safety audits, employers can ensure that following the agreed safety procedures becomes a natural part of the organisation's day-to-day operations. Employers may also wish to make health and safety part of the performance evaluation criteria for all employees. This means considering any hazardous incidents, near misses and instances of failing to comply with safety instructions and rules when evaluating the ongoing performance of all employees. As well as assessing safety compliance on an individual basis, the adherence of entire departments and teams to the safety rules should also be regularly assessed to ensure that employees are collectively and collaboratively following the agreed safe practices (Tanwar, 2023).

REFERENCES

Ali, Waqar (2021, August 18). Continuous Evaluation Of The Accountability System. https://www.hseblog.com/continuous-evaluation-of-the-accountability-system/

Angelo, Paul (2022, March 27). Safety Leadership: Foster a culture of accountability. https:// www.safetyandhealthmagazine.com/articles/22365-safety-leadership-foster-a-culture-of- accountability

Hanson, Eva Maria (2022, Dec 21). Implementing a food safety culture in 2023. https://www.fooddocs.com/post/food-safety-culture

Kello, John (2010, October 1). Positive Safety Cultures: Six steps to positive accountability. https://www.ishn.com/articles/90031-positive-safety-cultures-six-steps-to-positive-accountability

SafetyCulture Team (2018, Nov 30). We're all in This Together: Improving Safety Accountability in the Workplace. https://blog.safetyculture.com/safetyculture-news/improving-safety- accountability

Tanwar, Suresh (2023, March 07). Getting the culture right. https://www.britsafe.in/publications-and-blogs/safety-management-magazine/safety-management-magazine/2023/getting-the- culture-right/

Tanya (2020, February 6). 5 Steps to Change the Safety Culture in your Organisation. Https:// Www.Ecoonline.Com/Blog/5-Practical-Steps-To-Change-The-Safety-Culture-In-Your- Organisation

20

Rewarding Workers for Safety Cultural Change

Most organisations remain passive in celebrating employee rewards for safety culture, some are regularly active and integrate it to their appraisal process, yet sometimes rewards are unfair as perceived by employees which significantly and adversely affect the positive safety culture.

The research found that two forms of reward systems were most common, the hierarchy based system and the performance-based system. Each of these reward systems was examined in terms of how they help reinforce a firm's cultural values and norms. The relationship between growth strategy and reward systems was also studied. It was found that most firms with a steady-state growth strategy employed a hierarchy-based reward system, while firms with evolutionary growth strategies use performance-based reward systems (Kerr & Slocum, 2005).

Boyce (2018) observed that reward behaviours, not outcomes, to get the most value from safety incentives. Most organisations would be interested in safety outcomes which is achievable by behavioural science approach implementation.

Often people remain passive as there is no incentive or reward or recognition for the work that do. Cultural change requires that employees and associates are rewarded for each safety action they do for reducing the risks and hazards around and for safety of peers and colleagues. The goal of safety rewards and recognition programme is to encourage safe behaviour and discourage unsafe behaviour (Briggs, 2021).

It was observed that the experimental group's safety motivation and performance had improved (both for immediate and 1-month later performance). The results were further probed at Phase 3 (after 3 months), where it was found that the benefits of incentive and penalty (I/P) programmes were not long lasting and started replenishing. Findings of the study helped researchers conclude that safety incentives have only short-term influence on safety outcomes, while a long-term and permanent solution should be found (Ahmed and Faheem, 2021).

Jean Hill, Human Landing Systems (HLS) and Lander Ground Operations Design Systems Safety Reliability and Maintainability engineer, at Kennedy Space Center, received a "Yes, If" coin for continuously embracing the "Yes, If" approach in her work. Hill is willing to have the tough and honest conversations that address mitigations needed to ensure the HLS programme is meeting and identifying safety requirements. Safety culture's mission at NASA is to create an environment where everyone works safely, feels comfortable communicating safety issues, learns from mistakes and successes, feels confident balancing challenges and risks while keeping safety in the forefront, and trusts that safety is a priority (NASA, 2022).

Safety incentives have been practised for a long time in many industries and are an integral part of safety interventions. Contrary to the assumptions of managers and supervisors that material awards are particularly motivational, many employees preferred symbolic recognition, care by the company, the provision of training and professional development, and investment into improving their wellbeing, and a preference for collective recognition over individual rewards and discuss the values of certificates. Rewarding practices of companies should become more responsive to the individual wishes of employees and their specific socio-economic contexts and highlight the importance of employee involvement in reward programmes (Houette and Mueller-Hirth, 2022).

A safety incentive programme that includes safety awards, aka safety recognition and rewards programme, encourages employees to adhere to safety standards and regulations in the workplace. These programmes offer recognition (such as praise and formal awards) and rewards (like gift cards and company swag) to employees who demonstrate safe behaviour, such as hazard reporting or actively participating in safety training. They are designed to complement or enhance other workplace safety programmes and initiatives such as safety awareness and training programmes. A safety incentive or recognition and rewards programme helps build a positive safety culture in the workplace. They also encourage employees to work towards continuous improvement of health and safety in the workplace. The best safety incentive programmes are carefully planned to support company safety goals and objectives. However, they should be about more than just reducing incident rates. According to OSHA, safety incentive programmes should be carefully designed not to encourage under or over reporting. The most effective safety incentive programmes are based on leading indicators rather than lagging indicators. Safety incentive programmes based on leading indicators reward employees for safety-related behaviours and activities (such as taking steps to remedy unsafe situations or participating on a safety committee), rather than for results, e.g., zero incidents (Metron, 2023).

A safety incentive programme is a reward-based initiative used to encourage employees to meet and exceed safety standards in the workplace. Safety incentive programmes promote existing safety protocols and highlight effective safety processes performed by employees. These programmes reward employees with both tangible and intangible prizes once team members meet specified safety goals. Here are some ideas to help you initiate a safety incentive programme at your workplace: Consider using outside safety consultants, use incentives that aren't monetary, offer both rewards and recognition, create incentives that target your most-needed areas, Set high standards for safety incentives, consider all categories of employees, agencies and associates, use a safety incentive programme to complement, not replace an existing safety programme, initiate spot reward at the site for immediate praise of safe behaviour, make reporting a priority, reward employees on a regular and timely basis (Indeed, 2023).

There is a practice of incentives and rewards in safety culture movement, though the effects are limited, yet to maintain the safety climate, companies believe and act upon incentivising employees, as employees may remain unhappy in the absence of these rewards, however, they need such temporary mental stimulations as well as long lasting impact of personal recognitions for internal motivations for sustaining positive safety culture. Don't leave culture change to chance, create and manage it. Driving cultural change requires active and intentional leadership.

REFERENCES

Ahmed, Ishfaq and Faheem, Asim (2021). How Effectively Safety Incentives Work? A Randomized Experimental Investigation, Safety and Health at Work, Volume 12, Issue 1, 2021, 20-27, ISSN 2093-7911, https://doi.org/10.1016/j.shaw.2020.08.001.

Boyce, T. E. (2018, Apr 13). Safety Culture and Behavioural Safety. https://ehsdailyadvisor.blr.com/2016/08/reward-behaviours-not-outcomes-get-value-safety-incentives/

Briggs, Kelley (2021, May 12). How to implement safety incentive programmes using employee rewards and recognition. https://www.inspirus.com/blog/how-to-impliment-safety-incentive- programmes

Houette, Beate and Mueller-Hirth, Natascha (2022). Practices, preferences, and understandings of rewarding to improve safety in high-risk industries. Journal of Safety Research, Volume 80, 2022, 302-310, ISSN 0022-4375, https://doi.org/10.1016/j.jsr.2021.12.013.

Indeed (2023). 11 Safety Incentive Programme Examples (With Tips To Implement Them). https://www.indeed.com/career-advice/career-development/safety-incentive-programmes-examples

Kerr, Jeffrey & Slocum, John. (2005). Managing Corporate Culture Through Reward Systems. Academy of Management Executive. 19. 10.5465/AME.2005.19417915.

Metron (2023, March 2). Safety Awards, Rewards & Incentives for Building Strong Safety Culture. https://www.metronbranding.com/safety-awards/

NASA (2022, Feb 17). Safety Culture NASA, Safety Culture...It's in Our DNA. Https:// Sma.Nasa.Gov/Sma-Disciplines/Safety-Culture

21

Three Months E-Training Course: Questionnaire and Evaluation on "Behaviour Based Safety 2.0 (Zero-Harm with Positive Work Culture)"-Self-Study Each Chapter, Discuss with Mentor Dr HL Kaila

Six Steps for enrolment and completion of this e-course

1. Write to the author/mentor on kailahl@hotmail.com with your detailed purpose to join this course.
2. Minimum 20 sponsored participants (cross-functional leaders) are needed to enrol from an organisation/site.
3. 1st month: make course fee payment, receive e-course book/details, self-study all chapters, discuss each chapter in a weekly online session with the mentor Dr HL Kaila, an expert (positive safety culture implementation).
4. 2nd month: submit an individual assignment on 20 questions and answers.
5. 3rd month: make an online group presentation for developing action plan/ roadmap for implementation.
6. Course ends with an e-certificate signed by the mentor and your company /site head. Note: e-sessions link is to be sent by the sponsored company. This e-course can be customised for your company requirements.

This e-training has 20 questions, one from each chapter as below. The participant must go through each chapter above, answer each question in detail in your own language only, and then email all to kailahl@hotmail.com for evaluation. Each question carries 5 marks and total 100 marks. Each question must be answered in minimum 100 words for qualifying this test, copying and pasting the answer from Google like resources shall be the disqualification for this test. After this evaluation, open viva group presentation should be made by the participants to complete this e-course, in which, your company employees should actively participate as a learning exercise.

Chapter

1. *Safety, Health and Environment:* What is lacking in your organisation/site, and what is your action plan to fix the same? Please discuss the same with your team before answering.
2. *Future of Safety, Health and Environment:* What is the Future of EHS in your organisation. Critically review and discuss the same with your team and develop an action plan.
3. *Psychological Safety Culture:* Empower workforce to speak up for safety of each other, deeper insight is that let them speak up otherwise as well, for building a psychologically safe culture. Discuss this concept with your team for implementation issues involved in Psychological Safety Culture For Your Company and reply.
4. *Effect of BBS on Safety Performance:* Discuss the effects of BBS on safety performance with your team and reply with facts and data.
5. *Risk Perceptions:* Study this chapter, discuss and explain the issues involved in risk perceptions of your employees at your sites, and how would you manage the same?
6. *To Be A Global Company with Positive Safety Culture:* Companies before becoming a global entity, need to understand first that a positive safety culture is all about implementing a consciousness among the workers about the sense of brotherhood, affection, affiliation, support and

spot-correction of behaviours and barriers. Discuss your company scenario in this respect and reply after discussion with your team members.

7. *Resilient Organisations and Positive Safety Culture:* Developing resilient organisation and positive safety culture is meant to raise own implementation experience, data and information within the organisation so that it can bounce forward in case of incidents, failure or uncertainty. Discuss and reply after discussion with your team members.
8. *Managements Prioritise on the Safety Culture Drive:* Study this chapter, discuss and reply after discussion with your team members.
9. *Passion for Safety Culture Transformation:* Having a passion for safety means really actively caring about your people and your operations. If you take care of your people, they will be more productive. How would you implement passion for safety culture transformation amongst your employees?
10. *A Case on Positive Safety Culture:* Positive behaviour safety or big brother safety (BBS) provides the necessary components of care and timely intervention. However needs to be backed up by a robust safety management system. Discuss this in respect to your company scenario and reply in detail.
11. *Safety Culture Suffers From Disconnect and Decision Making:* Participation of employees in safety culture is less due to impaired felt leadership and dependent safety culture practised by site heads, top leaders, site leaders and frontline engineers. Explain this frankly and openly in reference to your company.
12. *Digitalisation of Positive Safety Culture:* Digitalising safety processes, checklists, training and implementations plays an essential role in driving your company's safety culture. Discuss your company practices in this regard for improvement to the next level.

13. *Success and Challenges of Positive Safety Culture:* A successful safety culture connects everyone around a common goal to measurably reduce near misses and incidents, and have huge implications for business success. Critically review this for your company's perspective.
14. *Total Safety Culture (TSC) Interventions:* A safety professional's goal is to achieve a TSC in an organisation including a good balance of enforcement and reinforcements between the interventions such as behavioural safety, psychological safety, human factors, human errors, cultural safety, and robust safety systems. Explain the above in reference to your company.
15. *Linking Safety Behaviour to Key Performance Indicators (KPI):* Like with one seed, we can grow thousands of fruits and more seeds, similarly with behavioural KPI of an individual employee and actions, we save thousands of lives from incidents, and prevent injuries innumerable. How would you implement this for your sites?
16. *Human Factors and Human Error in Safety Culture:* How your organisation and leadership responds to the human factors and human errors in building positive safety culture?
17. *Cultural Safety and Diversity (CSD):* How CSD is addressed to see that your workers at the lowest level are being listened to and understood with due respect to their cultural background, beliefs and language, for ensuring development of positive safety culture?
18. *Integrating Total Safety Culture Interventions with Organisational Behaviour:* Integrating and sustaining safety culture require a controlled focus on several levels of influence on worker safety and wellbeing, as the relationship between work and safety is never unidirectional. Explain this for your company scenario and implementation.
19. *Fixing Accountability Levels to Mobilise Positive Safety Culture:* Accountability, equality, encouragement, teamwork, and training are five elements of safety culture. All the five

work in tandem for building best work culture. Discuss your company's scenario in this regard.

20. *Rewarding Workers for Safety Cultural Change:* Most organisations remain passive in celebrating employee rewards for safety culture, some are regularly active and integrate it to their appraisal process. Explain your company's practices in detail on the above.

22

Behaviour Based Safety (BBS) 2.0: Integrate it as Company Value

Introduction

Analysis of accidents and incidents shows that human failure contributes to almost all accidents and exposures to substances hazardous to health. Many major accidents such as Bhopal, Chernobyl were initiated by human failure. In order to avoid accidents and ill-health, companies need to manage human failure or errors as robustly as the technical and engineering measures they use for that purpose (Health and Safety Executive, 2023). Human factors (positive or negative) are the organisational factors or situations that impact the people's actions and mindset. Supportive factors would reinforce safety culture, whereas the negative /reactive factors impede the safety behaviours of the workers. Managers and supervisors need to be trained to positively deal with stress and mental health issues of the employees for augmenting safety culture. Similarly, the situational factors like time pressure, fear, lack of resources create a mindset that nobody takes safety decisions, and safety culture takes a back seat, and incidents creep in taking toll on people and property (Lal, 2023). How organisations' leadership respond in such situations, matters most in re-building positive safety culture.

HSE professionals emphasised on balancing the challenges and issues while integrating the safety systems and positive safety culture. The elements of the total safety culture interventions must not exist as disjointed form in the organisation for best results of manpower safety as well as business prosperity. Safety systems provide nothing more than the safety climate. People need to feel psychologically safe for giving optimum performance. The complicated human factors of safety and the complex human error in safety must be addressed by the corporates. Cultural safety and equitable care require workers migrated from diverse cultural backgrounds to be understood in their own cultural backdrop, language and communication, so that any kind of racism or inequity is ruled out. Total safety culture framework integrates information across disjointed conceptualisations to clearly portray the dynamic nature of safety culture and specific drivers of its development.

BBS 1.0 & 2.0 is a journey from individual behaviours to organisational transformation. This chapter briefs on how behaviour based safety (BBS) 2.0 is implemented qualitatively/conversationally at organisational levels.

BBS 1.0 and 2.0 both together transform the safety culture into a positive work culture. BBS 2.0 focuses more on organisational culture factors, rather individual behaviour. BBS 1.0 is observational in nature, whereas BBS 2.0 is more conversational for developing response mechanisms to combat multifaceted organisational barriers while evaluating accountability of leaders for leading the positive safety culture intervention as a long-term roadmap for businesses.

How BBS 2.0 is implemented qualitatively and conversationally at organisational levels for establishing safety dialogues across the board from topmost level to the down-most/last person. It is important to fix accountability of each of the BBS steering teams interactions.

Defining BBS 2.0 Interventions

- *Behavioural safety:* behavioural interventions with long-term action plan/roadmap.
- *Psychological safety:* do people feel psychologically safe in an organisational context? Psychological safety is to be crucial for India Inc in 2023. 45% of all employers surveyed

believe that psychological safety is a strong performance indicator and 47% believe it is a crucial need since it leads to higher employee retention and engagement, according to new data (Sarkar, 2023).

- *Human factors in organisational cultural context:* do people feel very strained with occupational stresses, workload, decision latitude issues?
- *Human error in organisational cultural context:* human cognition, decision making, fear, pressure. How companies handle group conflicts and differences that delay safety culture decisions. The Bhopal tragedy and the IOCL Jaipur fire incident were the result of top level disengagement with the safety culture of their respective companies effecting into human error and poor decision making for actions needed to correct unsafe antecedents at sites. Human error is not personal error but in organisational cultural context. Errors are broadly classified into two kinds: latent and active errors. While active errors need to be addressed at the individual level, latent errors indicate organisational inadequacies (Vattipalli, *et al.*, 2021).
- *Cultural safety and competency:* do people feel being understood with due respect to their cultural background and beliefs, and how companies respond to these factors effectively? Cultural safety is more than the absence of racism, it is the positive recognition and celebration of cultures that empowers people and enables them to contribute and feel safe to be themselves (NSW, 2023).
- *Robust safety systems with digital intervention:* positively reinforcing antecedents for managing all safety issues such as barriers, resources, safety controls.
- Integrating and critical reviews by the topmost leaders on all the above six interventions towards a goal of vision zero-harm (Nambudiri & Ghulyani, 2018). Integrating and sustaining safety culture require a controlled focus on several levels of influence on worker safety and wellbeing, as the relationship between work and safety is never unidirectional.

Explain this for your company scenario and implementation. Characteristics of effective integrated interventions include the intervention development, implementation, and outcomes.

Basic difference between BBS 1.0 & 2.0 (BBS 2.0 does not replace BBS 1.0 but both are complementary to each other)

Culture building - Broad focus of BBS 1.0 is on	Perspective building - focus of BBS 2.0 is on
1. Observations and corrections	Increased open and empathic conversations across all levels, critical reviews, mass communications
2. Employees as observers at all levels/areas	Integrating contractors, customers, stakeholders
3. Individual behaviours	Organisational barriers/antecedents, resources provision
4. Corporate steering teams	MD level, Board of Directors reporting, challenge management's passionate involvement
5. Behavioural safety culture	Total safety culture: psychological safety, human factors, human error, cultural safety, digitalising, integration
6. Steering teams commitment for months/years	Accountability evaluation of leaders/managers, performance & policy based commitment for long term
7. Actively caring with empathy	HSE as core value and zero-harm, corporate rewards and reinforcements (digital and non-digital)
8. Quantitative score-board/ measurement	Qualitative site steering team/HoDs monitoring
9. Safety and business perspective	Health, safety, environment, well-being, sustainability
10. Monthly monitoring and recognitions	Weekly monitoring and spot-rewards at sites

Meeting Challenges of implementing behaviour based safety (BBS) 2.0

Although, an accountability of BBS steering teams at corporate and site location levels is fixed, there are challenges such as managers lacking challenges for long-term safety culture involvement. To deal with many such challenges, the following insights are shared below by industry leaders (Kaila, 2020, 2020a).

1. Journey of safety culture is 'from basics to core value by top management commitment' which opens benefits of BBS 2.0. Most companies plan safety culture intervention very scholarly but fail in driving it as a long-term change, due of lack of implementation of organisational factors. There are challenges such as not giving up the dependent safety culture by leaders, passiveness in mentally stimulating people down the levels, lack of reinforcement from respective HoDs/leaders, lack of skills in mobilising and involving all employees/associates (Lal, 2023).
2. *Core value of business:* Most of the managements do not have patience, actually there are no safety objectives in their business plans. Problem is when BBS is adopted as compliance-driven safety in place of commitment-driven safety. Then BBS becomes priority, not a core value of business. Priority can be changed due to dynamics of market conditions. Core value becomes a way of life. Still majority did not understand what would be the BBS impacts on organisational culture. It is perceived as an audit tool for monitoring behaviour attributes. There is a need for more in-depth understanding of BBS to bring on the table. Then only it can be a success. Initially, when starting BBS journey, the speed is very fast (like 70-80 kmph). Slowly, speed slows down due to less interest of management. People leave the organisation, or involve in different activities. To change the behaviour, provide planned infrastructure, monitor and enforce the safe practices, training and awareness, motivation both positive and negative. Companies take good initiative but fail due

to not getting right and strong leadership qualities in the team leaders and line managers. Secondly, the process is not watched and monitored as a long-term benefit. After some time, the process gets dissolved due to less attention and diversified focus. Safety can be implemented effectively when it will be a line function responsibility and part of routine activity. Management needs to discuss the safety parameters along with other operation parameters in routine meetings. For any project, it requires consistency and involvement from top management, without which such projects won't yield desired results (CPCL, 2021).

3. *Basic safety culture:* Safety culture fails in driving as a long-term change because of lack of basic safety culture in the organisation, like owning safety as if it is in every employee's DNA. For that, basic need is to be developed such as, use of PPE at site by all employees, top to bottom, every one has to know the safety policy, top management must involve in all safety activities, training is basic to develop safety culture, at least 3% of the man-hours should be consumed for employees' training, employees' feedback is very important, identification of hazard by execution or operation employees is the key, daily pre-job safety talk, etc. After settling in these basics, if these processes continue on their own without pushing, then we can establish safety culture, otherwise it will fall anytime.
4. *Top management:* Unless the top management is committed, nothing can be done. Commitment from top decides the safety culture. Management commitment is required to monitor change as a boardroom practice. As long as positive safety culture remains at doorstep of the boardroom, and does not find space and discussed sufficiently inside boardroom, it does not sustain. System works, but for long-term change, system has to be a part of behaviour which must be carried forward. It does not work due to lack of company's vision/policy (Kaila, 2022, 2022a).
5. O*rganisational politics or human error (oh god they do not know what they are doing):* Many companies begin well,

but due to latent organisational conflicts and group errors, they don't continue the positive safety culture. Hence, the BBS 2.0 intends that the organisational issues be resolved and corrected simultaneously for developing positive work culture. Passive and silent leadership on supportive safety culture is risky for businesses. Employees cannot be trained unless they implement, learn, and experience what they are trained for. More than an observation, conversation about the at-risk behaviours with the workers is important. Success of safety culture does not mean a destination, but it is a roller-coaster with ups and downs (Tata Steel, 2021).

Conclusion

Ten big reasons for un-sustainability of safety culture are that the companies are lacking in:

- Understanding workplace and psychological safety challenges, sharing of learnings.
- HoDs and all employees' understanding concepts deeply resulting in lots of unlearning.
- Steering team's adequate qualitative leadership for sustainability of safety culture.
- KPI for BBS to be added in management monthly presentation.
- Following timeframes of safety culture phases such as first 6 months in building BBS awareness, observation and structure. Next 6 months in strengthening reviews and accountability, etc.
- Maturity on part of organisation to promote psychological safety, particularly for leadership.
- Sowing the seeds of brotherhood: the foundation of safety culture which needs further manure.
- Feedback from all members in positive and constructive ways.
- Motivating self-regulations, observing self and mentoring, timely follow-ups.
- Linking BBS culture to safety systems, like consequences management, enforcement, etc.

Most companies take safety implementation as a face saving exercise to suit business perspective, because, the long-term commitment is a bit harder for them. Thus, they do their bit and sit back, to wait and watch for incidents. Some organisations set in a safety culture intervention, but did not continue as because they largely dwelt on individual behaviours, not the organisational behaviours. It is considered that the cluster of open conversations across all levels over a variety of organisational factors (such as rewards and relationships, perceptions and passions, beliefs and barriers, would recreate a new organisational behaviour pattern to follow on, implicitly put as BBS 2.0. The challenges of implementing BBS 2.0 are manifold as discussed in above section, but the chances of succeeding in safety culture would be maximised, as the focus is on the open conversations and dialogues about all the behaviours and antecedents related to safety culture in the organisation. If the employees feel that something new and positive in the organisation is going on, then it should continue over the years to become a norm, culture and a peoples' value. BBS, especially in its more recent incarnations, such as so-called BBS 2.0, go beyond a strict focus on reducing injuries (and often unfortunately blaming the victim) to take a more holistic approach that focuses not only on behaviours, but work environment, cultural antecedents, systems and employee attitudes to strengthen organisational cultures, values and performance (Johnson, 2021). The change in positive safety culture happens over the years and its sustainability need to be constantly explored. The management should continuously monitor and evaluate their strategies while delivering multifaceted interventions to be more specifically focused and to motivate workers to be enthusiastic in sustaining safety culture (Wong, *et al.*, 2021). Sembcorp Energy India Limited (SEIL) manages health, safety and environment (HSE) responsibility as its core value (SEIL, 2023a). To further strengthen the safety culture and secure a positive behavioural change within the workplace, SEIL has implemented and integrated BBS into its safety systems across all the assets. ISO 45001:2018 mandates that human competence and behavioural elements need to be considered in risk assessment and as an internal issue for managing risks (SEIL, 2023).

REFERENCES

CPCL (2021). CPCL kickstarts Behaviour Based Safety in Refinery at Chennai. https://cpcl.co.in/events-updates/cpcl-kickstarts-behaviour-based-safety-in-refinery-at-chennai/

Health and Safety Executive (2023). Human factors: Managing human failures. https://www.hse.gov.uk/humanfactors/topics/humanfail.htm

Johnson, Dave (2021, July 6).Breathing new life into Behavior-Based Safety (BBS) programs.https://www.ishn.com/articles/113027-breathing-new-life-into-behavior-based-safety-bbs-programs

Kaila, Harbans Lal (2020). Behaviour-Based Safety in Organizations: Life Before the Accident' I.K International Publishing House Pvt Ltd, New Delhi. ik_publishers@ikinternational.com

Kaila, Harbans Lal (2020a). TOP MANAGEMENT WILL to SUPPORT SAFETY CULTURE. International Journal of Research - GRANTHAALAYAH, Vol. 10 No. 4 (2022): Volume 10 Issue 4 : April 2022. DOI: https://doi.org/10.29121/granthaalayah.v10.i4.2022.4573

Kaila, Harbans Lal (2022). LONG-TERM SAFETY CULTURE Implementation. Prints Publications, New Delhi. ISBN-13: 9788192769462, https://www.printspublications.com/book/long-term-safety

Kaila, Harbans Lal (2022a). https://store.pothi.com/book/ebook-dr-harbans-lal-kaila-behaviour-based-safety-2-0/

Lal, H. (2023). Strengthening a positive safety culture despite underlying fear and peer pressure. World Safety Journal, XXXII(1), 57–64. https://doi.org/10.5281/zenodo.7770080

Nambudiri, Ranjeet & Ghulyani, Swati. (2018). GAIL (India) Limited: Transforming Safety Culture (Management Case: Ivey Publishing).

NSW (2023). What is cultural safety? https://www.safework.nsw.gov.au/safety-starts-here/our-aboriginal-program/culturally-safe-workplaces/what-is-cultural-safety Sarkar, B. (2023, Feb 15). Psychological safety to be crucial for India Inc in 2023. https://economictimes.indiatimes.com/news/company/corporate-trends/psychological-safety-to-be-crucial-for-india-inc-in-2023-and-beyond-survey/articleshow/97937736.cms?utm_source=contentofinterest&utm_medium=text&utm_campaign=cppst

SEIL (2023). Behaviour Based Safety (BBS) Implemented at SEIL. https://www.sembcorpenergyindia.com/CSR/BBS

SEIL (2023a). Safety at the Core. https://www.sembcorpenergyindia.com/AnnualReport2020/safety-at-the-core.php

Tata Steel (2021, March 15). Risk Profiling Turns Deep Shop Floor Experience into Enthusiastic Risk-Based Decision Making. https://www.consultdss.com/content-hub/risk-profiling-risk-based-decision-making/

Vattipalli Sameera, Bindra A, Rath GP. (2021). Human errors and their prevention in healthcare. J Anaesthesiol Clin Pharmacol. 2021 Jul-Sep;37(3):328-335. doi: 10.4103/joacp.JOACP_364_19. Epub 2021 Oct 12. PMID: 34759539; PMCID: PMC8562433

Wong SY, Fu ACL, Han J, Lin J, Lau MC. (2021). Effectiveness of customised safety intervention programmes to increase the safety culture of hospital staff. BMJ Open Qual. 2021 Oct;10(4):e000962. doi: 10.1136/bmjoq-2020-000962. PMID: 34625426; PMCID: PMC8504354.

Index